Stranded

Douglas Scott Delaney

Stranded

Copyright © 2023 by Douglas Scott Delaney
Cover Art by Barry Goldberg
Cover Design by Barry Goldberg and D. Bass
Book design & typesetting by D. Bass
ISBN: 979-8-218-11568-5

For further information, contact Coyote Web Synergy at: www.coyotewebsynergy.com

DEDICATION

This story is dedicated to anyone who ever thought
"It was a good idea at the time."

AUTHOR'S NOTE

I tell stories. It isn't a bad way to eke out a living. But I've been doing so for several decades now and whether I am working on a short story or a book or a play or a screenplay the percentage of truth in these stories will vary. My short stories and plays, though technically categorized as fiction, are usually about 90% non-fiction. They are all based on real people, real places and real events. In hindsight, I regret the 10% of Poetic License I employed in those tales, somehow thinking it made the work "better." Hindsight is simultaneously the most overused and underrated socket a writer keeps in his ratchet box. If I could go back into all my published fiction and produced plays I would gut the damn things, remove all embellishment, and let the truth of it stand alone. Call it evolution. Call it not wanting to bullshit anymore. Call it pure laziness. Whichever, I have discovered we all have stories in our lives that if told honestly and accurately, and without fear of retribution, need no embellishment. These are the stories we tell our kids. These are the stories we share around the kitchen table. These are the bus stop and bar stool stories. And the following is one of them. It started out with my kid asking me *Dad, did you ever go hitch-hiking?* Not thinking it would become the little monster it became, I began by posting a few pages on my social media (https://www. facebook.com/dsdelaniac) once a week. The response was as surprising as it was overwhelming. By the time the tale was told it had reached over 100,000 readers in every state and eleven countries. This was heady stuff. A lot of those kind folks asked if I would publish the series as a book. And here we are. Although I will say it has been revised and extended from the original version. Hence, the story to come. And when all is said and done it is just that—a story. But I hope it is one you will enjoy. And, in hindsight, it was a lot easier to tell it than it was to live it.

CONTENTS

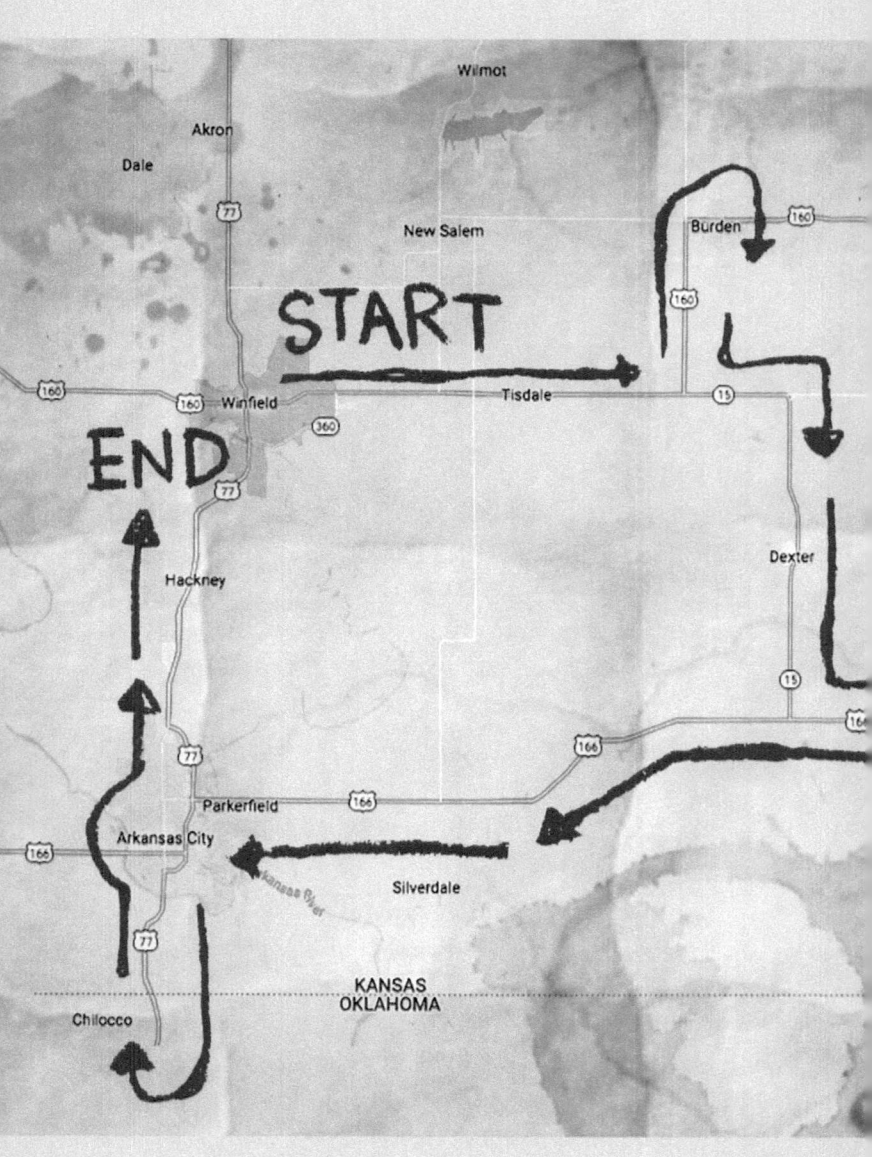

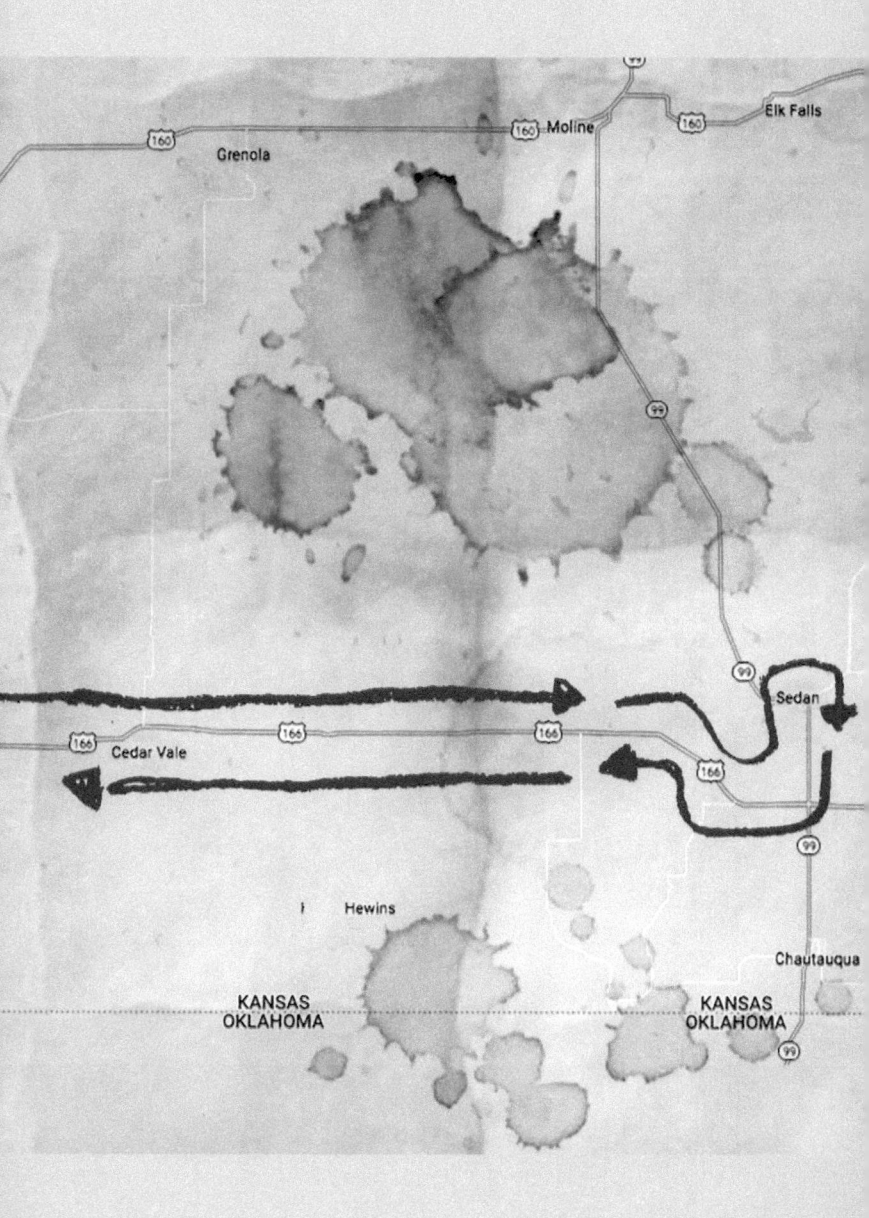

CHAPTER 1

IT'S RAINING CRAP

April 1978, Highway 160--Just East Of Winfield, KS

It was still Spring but out on the highway it was *hot*. I was on the shoulder of the road, sitting on my Dad's Green Beret duffel bag (which I had seriously over packed). I had on my best-worn 501s, my Frye Boots, my Dad's army jacket with all the Airborne patches....and my cowboy hat.

This wasn't *really* what any self-respecting cowboy would call a cowboy hat. It was my New York version of a cowboy hat, given to me by high school friends when they heard I was going to college in Kansas. It was more a farmer's hat, like the one Michael Landon always wore in *Little House On The Prairie*. And I would catch hell for that hat a few miles down the road.

I had 35 dollars in my pocket, no place to live for the next ten days and, as Chuck Berry so perfectly said it, *no particular place to go.*

I had been deposited on the shoulder of Highway 160 just outside the city limits by the Winfield Police Department about an hour earlier. They just didn't like the look of me hitch-hiking on Main Street. They were not rude nor mean. They just wanted me out of sight. So there I sat, wondering how the hell I got there.

This is how the hell I got there:

It was Spring Break. My fellow students were all gone down to Padre Island, Daytona Beach, the Colorado Rockies or to their home towns. The dorms were all closed. I was virtually broke and homeless. But I was not abandoned, not at first. Many of my pals invited me to go home with them, and even my folks offered to fly me home. But I turned all that down *because my girlfriend* invited me down to stay with her family in Ponca City, OK.

But, *then* my girlfriend, who shall remain nameless… (Know what? Screw that. Her name was Nancy Mathews). And Nancy Mathews thought it wise to inform me (the day before Spring Break) that she was no longer my girlfriend.

At this time I didn't even have the 35 bucks. It was my ol' college chum, Christopher *Kick'n K.C.* Klos (also known as *June Bug Boy*) who bailed me out. He earned his moniker by foolishly informing some of us in the dorm that he was deathly afraid of June Bugs. So we'd drop a few down the back of his underwear when the opportunity arose. He would shriek like a teenage girl and do this terrific little spastic ass-slapping dance all the way down the hall. It was cruel, yes, but we were freshman. Kick'n was having trouble in English Comp., basically failing, and since I was getting A's he offered to pay me 30 bucks, in advance, if I'd write his next term paper.

I told him, "Hell, for 30 bucks I'll get you a B minus, but for 50 bucks I'll get you an A plus."

The deal was struck. And I wrote the paper that night (after spending 15 bucks on beer and *Burger Station* burgers for the two of us). And the next morning Kick'n K.C. left for Kansas City and I left for well…destinations unknown.

And this is why:

I had been in Kansas since August of 1977 and I had seen none of the place, except the Wichita Airport and Winfield. Some friends had taken me to the city of Wichita one Saturday, but when we got there I kept asking them *exactly where this city was*. They said I was already *in* it. If I *was* in it I couldn't notice. It was unlike any city I had ever seen. It was more like a bunch of houses in search of a city. So I hadn't seen much. And, if when you got nuthin' you got nuthin' to lose, do something drastic. So I decided to turn my poverty, temporary homelessness and newly-busted heart into an adventure.

I would stand on the road until I got a ride and damn if I cared if I was headed East, West, North or South. The Winfield City Police decided that *for me* when they dumped me out on East Bound Highway 160. It was as good a highway shoulder as any.

It was *fate*.

It was *kismet*.

Because on the very first morning of my big adventure I got picked up by two of the most profoundly insane people I have ever met.

Meet Karl and Jubal. Both in their late 20s. I was 18. They pulled up in a big, black smoke belching, dually diesel pick-up. It used to be white but was now covered in grease and oil and mud and *godknowswhat* else. They were oil field roustabouts (their coveralls soaked in oil and sweat) wearing filthy "gimme" caps and pointy-toed boots.

Karl was driving and Jubal was sitting beside him on the single bench front seat. Jubal leaned out the window and shouted to me, because that truck hadn't seen a muffler in years and it sounded like erratic artillery fire.

"Hey, Son!" Jubal yelled. "You a COWBOY?!"

"NOPE!" I replied.

"Then hop on in here you sonofabitch --'cause we HATE cowboys!"

And I did. And off we went. Me on the right, Jubal in the middle, and a Gott Tote 18 Cooler filled with Buck Horn beer between he and Karl. Judging by the pile of empty cans at my feet, these two had been at it a while.

They had gotten off shift at 6:00 A.M., drove down to Oklahoma for some 6.0 beer. "Not that 3.2 CRAP you gotta' buy in Winfield!" And they were heading back home "up Moline way" for a weekend of fishing and drinking and hunting and drinking and carousing and drinking and...

These boys had a plan.

And being Kansans, they of course invited me along to share in their diversions. And I was all for that, being the bold adventurer. Highway 160 broke hard left (or North) toward Burden, which was about five or six miles up the road. And it was in that five or six miles that I came to the conclusion that come hell or high water I had to get away from Karl and Jubal as soon as friggin' possible. Because aside from their Good Ol' Boy charm and easy manner, their half-shaven, grinning faces and their six point Buck Horn Beer--Karl and Jubal also had explosives.

And they liked to use them.

When I say *explosives* I am not talking Black Cat 'Crackers and Cherry Bombs. I am not even talking M-80s. I am talking big, fat red sticks of dynamite with fuses and blasting caps. And about every half mile or so, when a target of opportunity arose, Karl would squeal and skid onto the shoulder, and Jubal would run on out and…

BOOM!!!!!

…blow the hell out of something.

And they hooted and hollered like giddy children at every big bang.

They blew up an old farm stand about 40 feet off the road.

They blew up an old outhouse outside an abandoned Quonset Hut.

And (and this is my favorite) they blew up a huge pile of manure just sitting there on a concrete pad.

"WE ARE SURE IN THE SHIT NOW!" Jubal shouted, as aromatic chunks of cow crap rained down upon the truck and highway like fat dollops of stinking mud.

And then Karl leaned over to me and handed me a half–a-stick of dynamite and said, "You wanna' give it a go?"

Did I want to give it a go?

I was quaking in my Frye boots, about to pee my 501s, and this cornpone freaking maniac wants to know if I want to "give it a go?!"

"No, thanks, " I said. "But you go ahead."

"Probably for the best," Karl said. "This shit is pretty dangerous."

When we pulled into Burden, KS (population 512) and not a one of them anywhere to be seen, I "suddenly remembered" I had "friends" here and I'll be *getting out now,* thank you.

"NOBODY has friends here," Jubal said, smiling with big Skoal-stained teeth. "They might got relatives but they ain't got friends. But suit yourself, Son, and best of luck to ya'."

And off they went, blowing that black smoke and tossing Buck Horn beer cans out both windows. Wherever they were headed I was sure they were gonna have a good old time and I was also damn sure they were gonna have it without me, thank God.

It was barely 10:00 A.M. And I had gone exactly 18.6 miles.

And I stood on the Main Street of Burden, KS (Now Pop. 513) and not a sole was in sight. Not a car, not a truck, not a tractor, not a dog or cat. Nobody was home in Burden that day.

But there seemed to be two businesses open. A bar and a bank. And as I pondered the next phase of my big adventure I thought about how quite possibly, for the rest of my born days, I will *never* on this earth meet anybody quite like Karl and Jubal.

And know what? I sure as shit have not.

So I went into this little bar and it was so dark inside I was frankly blind. And before my eyes could adjust someone shouted out

"HEY! You a COWBOY, Son?!"

CHAPTER 2

BUBBAS ONE & TWO

I wasn't inside that little bar two seconds (my big duffel bag on my shoulder and my hat tipped back on my head) before someone inside made that crack about my hat.

"HEY! You a COWBOY, Son?"

And I thought, *Oh, Christ, here we go.*

There was just *something* about that hat that encouraged such inquiries. I wasn't any cowboy. And I didn't pretend to be a cowboy. And I had met, oh, about 1000 people in Kansas who wore cowboy hats and they *damn* sure were not cowboys. As a matter of fact, there was only one person I have ever met that WAS a cowboy, but I'll get to him in a minute.

I just stood there in this NO NAME BAR, taking in this dark, stale-beer smelling place, which was slowly coming into focus.

"I *said*," he said, "Are you a COWBOY, Son?"

And then another voice said, "Are you a REAL cowboy?"

Usually, when commenting on my hat people were very good natured. But I could tell by the tone in these two that they were being very condescending, very…well…they were being assholes, to be precise.

Stranded

And if I had anywhere else to go at that moment I would have just turned around and walked right out, because I knew whatever this WAS was gonna get worse the moment I opened my mouth and in my Brooklyn, New York accent said, "I'll have a beer."

So I said, "Can I have a BEAH?" exaggerating my own accent just to get it over with.

And we were off.

"Well, I'll be DAMNED," one of them said. "We got us a NOO YAWK, COWBOY!"

And hilarity ensued. They just thought that was the funniest damn thing they had ever heard.

As they guffawed I took in the place and realized this establishment was about as much of a "bar" as my hat was a "cowboy hat." It was more like being in the kitchen of a crappy double-wide.

It had a couple of short pub tables with mis-matched chairs and a 6' long piece of wood as the "bar." And there was an open doorway, covered by a dingy curtain. And when it blew open a few times I could see through to a room where some old man was sitting in a recliner, eating soup off a folding tray and watching *The Price Is Right* on a black and white portable TV.

I also finally got a good look at the two jokesters. Both in their 50s, I guessed, all flannel and denim, and sporting John Deere caps. They were still chuckling at their own cleverness as the stout woman behind the plank slid me a Bud.

"Hey, NOO YAWK," one of them said, eyeing my duffel bag. "Whacha' doin' here?"

I said, "Just passing through," and I regretted *that* the split second the words left my mouth. I had just used one of the *most common cowboy clichés ever uttered* and that sent them off on another round of laughter.

And now I was getting a bit pissed off. It had been a rough morning already. And what was so damn funny about me to these guys was puzzling. I figured they were either very easily amused or very frigging drunk. And it turned out to be both. But either way I wasn't in the mood for it. So I stood up, pulled my hat over my eyes and paraphrased a line from *The French Connection 2* that seemed appropriate for the occasion.

"Listen *Y'all*," I said, "I'd rather be a lamppost in NOO YAWK than the fucking Mayor of Burden, Kansas."

And that shut them up but good.

The seconds that now passed seemed like hours while I waited for them to stand up, adjust their belts and throw me out onto that barren, dusty Main Street.

But instead, they started laughing again, this time heartier and louder than before. They verily exploded, laughing till they coughed and had to catch their breaths.

"You got THAT right!" one of them said.

And the other said, "Sit down here, boy. We're just funnin' ya'."

They waved over to the stout woman to bring us a round of beers and we sat and chatted for hours. And they wouldn't let me pay for a single beer. They told me that being a new face in town they felt it was their civic duty to bust my chops, just something they kinda' liked to do around there.

We dispensed with official introductions. They called me NOO YAWK and I called them BUBBA 1 and BUBBA 2.

We even swapped hats for a bit.

They listened, though, to my tale of woe, and informed me that if I didn't want to hitch-hike anymore that day and they had a hotel right there in town. That was odd because I didn't see any hotel and told them so.

"Well, it ain't much of a hotel, " Bubba 1 said. "And it sure as shit don't *look* like a hotel."

"But it IS a hotel," Bubba 2 said. "Call it the St. Elmo. Gotta see the Lady at the Bank to get a room."

"But you gotta get there before the bank closes at five," said Bubba 1.

And I am sitting there thinking *Where in the hell have I just landed?* I got to see the Bank Lady before five to get into the hotel that don't look like a hotel but IS?

My only food that day at the bar was microwave pizza which tasted like cardboard and ketchup and a few bags of three year old potato chips. But it was something. And though I really did want to head on down that lonesome highway the beer and idleness was making me tired.

Decisions, decisions.

While I was making up my mind the talk turned to cowboys again. BUBBAS 1 and 2 informed me there really aren't any *real cowboys* left about unless you count the rodeo kind. And that flipped a switch in my head.

I *knew* a rodeo cowboy!

His name was Merle Krug, a fellow Southwestern College student.

And Merle Krug rode bulls.

I told them that and they went about ape shit.

"You know Henny Krug?" Bubba 1 said.

"I know a *Merle* Krug," I said.

And Bubba 2 said, "Same thing! Hell, Boy, had we'd a *known* that we wouldn'ta give you so much shit!"

"Henny is *from* here!" Bubba 1 said. "Now that boy's a *real* cowboy."

The Lady at the bank (who looked and dressed like a Bank Lady) indeed was the lady that owned the hotel. And after charging me eight dollars for the room she escorted me to the St. Elmo. (Which was as much of a hotel as my hat was a cowboy hat and that bar was a bar.)

It was a two-story stone building with a creaking front porch, built in 1889 and showing all the signs of just that. Inside the main "lobby" was a dark wooden stairway. There was one door off the lobby and looking inside I could see it led to some kind of apartment. A sullen, dingy place with cheap, warped paneling and a curling, yellowing linoleum floor. And I realized this place was probably more of a boarding house now than a hotel.

It very well could have been one of the last of its kind.

My room upstairs had a huge soft bed, a slat-back chair, a window open to a dirt alley and a 7 foot tall cedar wardrobe.

Before she left I asked the Bank Lady if anyone else was staying there and she said

"Just Truman. He lives downstairs. Kinda' like a tenant more than a guest."

"Okay," I said.

"Don't mind him if he gets to 'fussin," The Bank Lady said, "He's pretty much harmless."

And she left. And I lie on the bed. And after about five minutes I shot up in bed thinking *Pretty much harmless*?

About 2:00 A.M. I was awakened from a sound sleep by what sounded like the howling of a wounded animal writhing in agony.

I had *never* in my life heard anything like it and it scared me shitless.

This was accompanied by the slamming of doors and the crashing of glass.

I opened my door (which I just then realized had no lock) and squinted down the stairwell, where I could see convulsive, jerking shadows fluttering in the lobby and still hear that woeful moaning.

I went from scared shitless to absolutely terrified.

I slammed the door. I slid the huge 7 foot wardrobe in front of the door and sat in the chair by the opened window, figuring if I had to I could just jump the hell down into the dirt alley and run for my young life.

Truman had come home.

And he was *a fussin'*.

CHAPTER 3

BAYONETS, BOOKS
& THE BRUNER BROTHERS

I sat trembling by the window in my second story room at the St. Elmo Hotel in Burden, KS, deciding whether or not to jump out and run for my life.

This was because there was what I deemed to be a mad man carrying on downstairs: breaking glass (bottles I assumed) shuffling about, slamming doors, and muttering indecipherable oaths against humanity.

According to the Bank Lady who rented me this room, the only other person in this hotel was someone named Truman, who apparently was drunk, clinically insane or turning into a werewolf.

It was about 2:00 A.M. and I had been on the road for about 16 hours on my *Discovering Kansas Hitch-Hiking Trip* that was supposed to last 10 days. I was already down to 25 bucks and was woozy with exhaustion. And after I barricaded my door with the huge wardrobe, I realized this would be a very sleepless night indeed.

Even at 3:00 A.M. when all the downstairs commotion seemed to subside, I knew I would not get a wink of sleep and decided to brave the stairway and get the hell out of there.

I slid the wardrobe over, shouldered my duffel bag, put on my *Hat of Contention*, opened the door, and started down that 100 year old wooden staircase, walking on egg shells 'cause those steps screeched like a cat in heat.

In the lobby I noticed that the door to Truman's apartment was open and there he sat at the kitchen table, a single dim light bulb swinging over his head, a bowl of decaying fruit in front of him.

He was old but I couldn't say how old. I was 18, so anyone over 40 was old. But he was at least in his 60s or 70s. He was decked in flannel and overalls, his hair a tufted mess and sporting a few days' worth of scraggly beard.

And we just stared at each other, like two gunslingers waiting for the other to make the first move.

And he did make the first move.

He pulled put a bayonet from his lap and pointed it at me.

And then, ever so quietly, he said to me, as if these words explained his entire situation:

"Malmedy."

All I could think to say was, "Okay."

And then he said, "Nazi Bastards shot me in the ass."

I really had no response for that. And for raising such a ruckus earlier, he suddenly looked very small and indeed, as the Bank Lady had said…harmless.

"Damn, it was cold," he said, then took his bayonet and began to cut up apples.

And I hit the lonesome blue highway once again.

In pitch black, I headed back South toward 160. My only other option was to continue West toward Moline, but that is where Jubal and Karl (*The Dynamite-ic Duo*) lived and I really did not wish to revisit that kind of instability.

Not a single car or truck passed by, and I walked the five or six miles until I reached the 160-K-15 junction. By now my duffel bag (which I seriously over-packed) was cutting deep creases into my shoulder and I started throwing things away: books, clothes, back-up sneakers. What the hell was I thinking when I packed this thing? Why did I bring *books*?

At the junction I dropped my bag and lie back against it, a few feet off the shoulder in the short, dew-moistened grass. And it was here I marveled at how absolutely *dark* was the Kansas Night.

It was as black as a bull's heart.

And coming from Long Island, where there was always a light on somewhere, I had never seen the stars like I saw them that early morning. There seemed to be billions of them. And I guess there were.

And I fell asleep, dreaming of a warm bed and *Burger Station* burgers smothered in onions and when THAT CAR HORN blew I leapt up like a frog on a hot plate.

I was in instant fight or flight mode, thinking I was back in the St. Elmo Hotel and Truman was hacking through my door with his bayonet.

And then, shuddering awake, I saw big smiling faces staring at me from inside that car. And after a second I realized they were two very familiar smiling faces.

It was "Big" Brad Bruner and his brother Greg "Turk" Bruner, both students and basketball players back at

Southwestern College in Winfield. And while Turk just shook his curly blonde hair and laughed, Big Brad said, "*WHAT in the WORLD* are you doing out here?"

So, I told them. I told them about being dumped by Nancy Matthews, and being locked out of the dorm and the *Dynamite-ic Duo* Karl and Jubal and the Ball-Busting Hat Squad from the Burden Bar and, of course, about Truman, the misaligned.

They stared at me in disbelief. Then at each other. And being brothers, you could tell they could read each other's minds without saying a word.

And then Turk said, "Christ, Delaney, *you're* coming with US."

This was not an offer so much as it was a demand.

And off we went. West on 160, West toward Sedan, West toward their hometown.

These were upper classmen, and just two really nice guys and I admired them. Big Brad's girlfriend worked at the after-hours snack bar in the student union at S.C. and (with a nod and a wink from Big Brad) she was always good for sliding us starving freshmen a free plate of fries or a fountain coke.

And Turk was just as amicable. Just damn nice good old Kansas "Boys," and also really terrific basketball players. And they had no explosives, bayonets or wise-cracks about my hat, either.

I think they enjoyed me because to them I was such an oddity. There was nothing special to them about these wide open spaces and highways they had traveled all their lives. But to me it was like a trip to the moon. Besides the ocean,

I had *never* seen such openness and beauty in my life. And every mile held a new revelation.

"Look," I said, "cows!"

"Yeah," Big Brad said. "We got some cows."

"Look," I said, "That plane's blowing smoke."

"That's a crop duster," Turk said.

We rode through Dexter, Cedar Vale, Wauneta…

This was their plan: They were going to stop at their mom's for the night and then head off to go camping and fishing at Lake Of The Ozarks in Missouri. And, of course, being Kansans, they invited me to come along.

And I wanted to say:

Yes! Sweet Jesus Mary And Joseph Hallelujah! Yes! Save Me From This Road Trip From Hell I Have Embarked Upon! Thank You! Thank You! Thank You!"

But there were two problems with saying that.

1. I was down to 25 bucks and no way I could afford an extended camping trip: the food, the beer, the bait, the license. I just could not pay my own way and though I *knew* they didn't give a damn about that, I did.

2. This was indeed a seminal, formative moment in my life. I had set out to do *something* and come hell or high water I was going to do what I set out to do. Even if it killed me. This was a matter of pure testosterone-tinted, teenaged, bull-headed pride.

And I thought that would garner at least a smidgen of admiration from Big Brad and Turk Bruner.

It didn't.

When I asked them to just drop me off in downtown Sedan, they both admonished me for being "a crazy, stubborn, New York asshole," and I *did* take some pride in that.

But just before they pulled away Turk leaned out the window and said, "You need any money?"

And I said, "No."

And they were not a half a block away before I *completely regretted* not going with them.

So, once again, I walked to the nearest intersection in downtown Sedan (population 1500) sat on my duffel bag and got out my map. I had the usual four choices: North, South, East, West.

Being from Back East I decided to head Back West, and after only a few minutes a woman (30s perhaps) in a really nice pickup truck, pulling a horse trailer, stopped for me.

"I'm only going as far as Cedar Vale," she said.

And I said, "That would be great."

If Merle Henny Krug (my Burden connection) was indeed a COWBOY, then this woman was definitely a COWGIRL. She wore tight, faded, dusty jeans. She wore mud covered boots and a wrinkled white cotton, collared shirt. She had crazy long jet-black hair ribboning down from her battered straw *real* cowboy hat. She had a Marlboro Red cigarette dangling from her lips and a Long Neck Bud between her legs.

And, well *hell*. Screw *you*, Nancy Mathews.

I was in love.

CHAPTER 4

I SEE EYES OF BLUE & SKIES OF GREEN

I had been on the road for a little over 28 very crowded hours and I had gone less than 60 miles. I had slept less than two hours on the side of KS-160 in the dewy grass, under the brilliant star-lit Kansas Sky. And all the lunacy of Karl and Jubal and the Bubbas and Truman and Big Brad and Turk were blasted into insignificance as I fell instantly and madly in love with this gorgeous cowgirl the nanosecond she pulled up alongside me and uttered those immortal words: "I'm only going as far as Cedar Vale."

I wished to hell Cedar Vale was about 1000 miles down that Blue Highway, but I knew it was less than 20 because I had already been through it earlier. So little time, so much woman! And her eyes—a *steely, cobalt blue*. Dark and mysterious.

Her name was Casey and she was just so damn adorable and sexy in that cowgirl *don't give a damn way*. And, being maybe 28-30, she was an "Older Woman."

Be still my 18 year-old palpitating heart.

At this point I must mention that my experience with women at this time was virtually nil. I had known some girls, like the one who just dumped me (thank you, once again

Nancy Mathews) and my high school sweetheart, Maureen, but these were *girls*. And really, I was just a *boy* myself.

But Casey was a whole 'nother thing. And in my inherent awkwardness with females of all ages I struggled to think of something witty, engaging and profound to say. But after turning down her offer of a Long Neck Bud and a Marlboro, all I could come up with was

"You got horses back there?"

And without missing a beat, she said

"No…hamsters."

She said it with such a straight face that my synapses could not fire fast enough to realize it was sarcasm.

Then she said, "That was sarcasm."

And myself, razor-harp wit at the ready, replied

"Oh."

"Of course, there are horses back there," Casey said. "You like horses?"

"Yes," I said, "I think so. But they don't like me."

Casey's face then filled with concern, as if that was just the saddest damn thing she had ever heard. And I could tell she wanted to know more.

So I explained to her that coming from the Brownstones of Park Slope, Brooklyn and the Popcorn Houses of Long Island Suburbia, my experience with horses was limited to one really bad experience at an oversized Petting Zoo called The Long Island Game Farm.

It was there, when I was ten, that I posed for a photograph with a horse. I was shirtless. And when I put my arm around that horse's neck it dropped its head and bit me in the chest, actually drawing blood.

"Ouch!" Casey said.

But, though seemingly sympathetic to my equine horror story, I could she was stifling a laugh, squeezing her lips shut, trying not to crack up.

"Bit you in the chest?" she said.

"Yes. It hurt like hell."

"It bit you in the nipple, didn't it?" she said, more a statement than a question.

"Yes," I said, amazed. "*How did you know?*"

"It thought it was an apple," she said. "Trust me, I know."

Here is where my mind begins to race as fast as my longing heart.

TRUST ME I KNOW?

Did she get her nipple bit by a horse who mistook *that* lovely attribute *for an apple*?

If so, *how*?

Did she run around the corral topless??

Oh, please God let that be true.

While I was still working on *that* little scenario in my head I heard the shoulder gravel crunch under the tires as Casey pulled over at the intersection of Highway 166 West and County Road 3, which was all rock and dust.

"Here is where I get off," Casey said. "You don't got a lot of choices. Stay on the blacktop and you got Ark City about 30 miles down. You take the gravel you got…well… you got nuthin' but Oklahoma."

As I was wrestling my duffel bag out of the back seat she said

"*Or…*"

(And that "*Or*" still lingers in my head to this day.)

"Or," Casey said, "You could learn not to be afraid of horses."

I can't remember whether we headed North or South on County Road 3, but when we got to Casey's there sat a modest, white clapboard house with a large, covered porch, and several outbuildings, including a four-stall stable and a corral fenced in by welded wire and steel posts, and topped with soft, black dirt.

And there Casey taught me the rudiments of how to act around a horse. How to move a horse from A to B. How the back end of a horse was far more dangerous then the front end.

"I'd rather get bit by a horse any day than *kicked* by one," Casey said.

Just like Big Brad And Turk Bruner, Casey seemed more bemused by me than anything else. And I learned she was just doing her duty as a Kansan and humanitarian in not letting me go another mile down that road being afraid of the very things she loved.

And any thought of romance I had still poking me in the brain went POOF when out of the house comes this *man,* this *big man* (bigger than Big Brad by a head) this big handsome, toothsome Marlboro Man--Stetson, mustache and all.

He kissed Casey on the cheek, gave me the once-over, extended his hand and said, "Well, what do we have here?"

When he shook my hand he looked me dead in the eye. His grip was like an anaconda.

After the pleasantries, he said, "You gonna stay and eat?"

And me, though starving, and having my heart on the chopping block twice now in two days, politely declined.

"I really ought to get on down the road," I said, stoically, as if I actually had someplace to go.

And Marlboro Man drove me back to 166.

I walked from County Road 3, through soft and sleepy Cedar Vale, and sat on my duffel bag on the East Side of town, not even sticking out my thumb.

And there I saw a rusted old sign filled with bullet holes.

And I remembered how that morning I had seen a similar sign just outside Sedan, right after the Bruner Brothers dropped me off.

It said:

WELCOME TO SEDAN, KS POP. 1579
HOME OF EMMETT KELLEY

Emmett Kelly! Even in my youthful ignorance I knew that man to be the most famous clown in American History. And I had to laugh.

Now Kansas Highway 166 could boast of *two* clowns.

And that is when the sky just opened up. It came out of nowhere, as Kansas Storms are wont to do. Black and purple clouds just tumbled all over each other like Sumo Wrestlers and the wind was outrageous and the rain was unrelenting daggers. Lightning crackled and flashed and I ran like hell toward a small, abandoned barn just a few yards off the road.

I stood in the big, open door way and marveled at the power of this frigging maelstrom. And then I saw something I had *never seen in my life* and have rarely seen since.

If you could look though those clouds and rain and lightning you could see that

THE SKY WAS GREEN!

A GREEN SKY!!!!

HOLY COW! WHAT A DAY! CASEY, HORSES AND A GREEN SKY!

And in just a few minutes Marlboro Man pulled up, honking, and waved me into his truck.

"Casey got all worried about you," he said, putting the truck in gear and heading West down 166 toward Ark City.

"Thank her for me," I said.

"My sister's like that," Marlboro Man said. "She picks up strays like an ol' Mother Hen."

WHAT?

WAIT!

SISTER?

Marlboro Man popped a beer and handed it to me. And I wondered if he could see the tiny, hopeful smile on my face: that down that lonesome, storm-tossed Kansas highway, hope sprang eternal in more places than one.

CHAPTER 5

BOOMER SOONER

It was just pushing two or three in the afternoon when the Marlboro Man delivered me to the South Side of Arkansas City, Kansas at the intersection of Highways 166 and 77.

The rain had stopped. I was still only on the second day of my 10 Day Spring Break Hitch-hiking adventure and I had gone less than 100 miles, pretty much in a flattened circle, like a paramecium.

I had *come to look for America* and so far I hadn't seen much of it outside of three tank towns, a lot of blue highway, one hell of a thunderstorm and some really, *really* fascinating people, ranging from the down-home quirky to the certifiably insane to the phenomenally desirable.

I had 8 days to go, 25 bucks, and not a clue as to what to do next. Though my finances looked bleak, my options, oddly enough, were unlimited. I could go as far as the kindness of strangers would allow.

So, being just about 4 miles from the Kansas-Oklahoma Line, and being I had *never* been to Oklahoma, I decided to go to Oklahoma, "where the corn is as high as an elephant's eye."

Stranded

But there was no corn. Just more miles and miles of low, barely rising hills and sporadic traffic, none of whom chose to help a brother out.

But still—a *new state*! Land of Woody Guthrie and Will Rogers! Boomer Sooner!

What wonders awaited me!

Actually…None.

Why I thought Northern Oklahoma would be any different from Southern Kansas is beyond me, but I did. It made even less sense when thoughts of home reminded me that though the whole country might think there is a big difference between N.Y. and New Jersey (just between us) there really isn't.

But tell *that* to New Yorkers and New Jerseyites and them's fightin' words. And my experience at Southwestern College also taught me there was no small amount of vitriol between the Jayhawks and the Sooners. I think this was and is a matter more of attitude than geography: the intrinsic America tendency to establish here-to-fore nonexistent boundaries and then get into pissing matches over them.

State lines…railroad tracks…picket, chain link and barbed wire fences…all great reasons to drop the gloves and go at it.

Arkansas City, which was just to the North at my back, is a perfect example of that. It was Arkansas City (ARK-AN-SAW) long before Kansas became a state. But when Kansas *did* become a state some outbreak of civic pride resulted in renaming ARK-AN-*SAW* City… AR-*KANSAS* City.

26

Same with the Arkansas River. Colorado, Oklahoma and Arkansas call that river the ARK-AN-*SAW*. But from the time it hits Kansas way out west and leaves Kansas just a few miles to my left as I walked South on 77, it is the AR-*KANSAS* River.

To each his own. But this *still* was a serious thing, because I had been corrected about 600 times already when I "mispronounced" Arkansas the same way the populations of 49 other states did.

And I wondered if people in Little Rock called Kansas Kan-*SAW*.

I had been walking down 77 South and was only maybe five or six miles into Oklahoma, just North of Newkirk, where I came upon what I can only describe as a *roadhouse* on the West side of the highway.

It was little more than a shack (and I cannot recall the name) but I did know of this place. It was where Kansans went when the 3.2 beer bars in their state closed at midnight, and they weren't quite through for the evening.

The bar itself was closed but there was a circular, gravel driveway looping behind the place, where there was a Drive-Thru Window, and that *was* open. There was a little plastic doorbell button jerry-rigged on the outside and I pushed it.

A grungy steel box slid out of the wall and a disembodied voice said, "What do you need?"

I ordered a six-pack of 6.0 beer and sat at a warped and creaking picnic table back by a copse of trees. And there I saw the most unusual and inventive urinal I had ever seen.

It was right out in the open—a series of 8" channel iron sections on wooden stilts about two feet off the ground, like a trough. The first section ran parallel to the gravel drive and then made a hard left, where it disappeared into the woods.

Don't people pee inside around here? I thought.

And then I postulated that it made perfect sense. The owners of this place were probably sick and tired of already beer-sodden Kansans driving down from Winfield and Ar-*KANSAS* City in the wee hours and hopping out of their cars to take a leak in their parking lot.

After a few beers, I availed myself of this innovation and it worked perfectly. I had come to look for America, and now I was peeing into a Rube Goldberg Contraption made from scratch and a little imagination--how perfectly American such an endeavor.

As far as Oklahoma was concerned (and though I was sure there was a lot more to the state than this) I had had enough and hauled my duffel bag back to 77 and stood on the Northbound side and it wasn't two minutes before a woman in a late model four-door sedan pulled up.

"I'm headed to Winfield" she said, and I guess so was I.

Back to the egg. What the hell.

Her name was Beulah, possibly in her late-50s, and she was all smiles and Okie Twang. She was headed to work the 2nd Shift at Gott Manufacturing, where she ran the inspection line.

If you've ever seen a Gatorade Dump in any NFL Game you know what Gott made-- because it was in Winfield all those orange coolers were designed and created before they were bought out by Rubbermaid.

We drove through Ark City, a *lonnnnnng* town, and then another 14 miles to the South Side of Winfield. I had Beulah drop me off at the Sonner Motor Lodge on Main Street. It was built in that 1960s Howard Johnson's motif, and it was more wishful thinking than reality because I knew I could not afford the place, and I was right. They wanted 22 bucks and I was now down to 21.

What to do, what to do.

I didn't have much time to ponder *what to do* because I wasn't 50 feet down Main Street from the Sonner Motor Lodge when the *same damn Winfield city cop* that escorted me out of town the day before pulled up and beckoned me to his driver side window.

"Back so soon?" he said.

Having no real answer I clicked into wise ass mode.

"I figured you missed me," I said.

And to my surprise he laughed and motioned me to *get in the car.*

He pulled a U-Turn on Main, but instead of taking me to the outskirts of town like he had done before, he made a right just before the Sonic and crossed the railroad tracks where the road then turned to gravel.

"I can't have you wandering all over town, you know," he said.

I then explained to him my situation. Busted plans… broken heart…locked out of dorm….21 bucks, etc.

He drove about a mile down the gravel and pulled over at the Tunnel Mill Dam, a horseshoe bend in the Walnut River.

There were fishermen and campers and picnic tables and BBQ grills. There were tall trees and raging water.

He then took out a notepad from his shirt pocket and started to write. He handed me the note, which had his signature on the bottom.

"Look," he said, "*This* is your Camping Permit. Behave."

After I got out he rolled down his window and said, "Get a job or something. I'm tired of lookin' at you."

This could work, I thought. I *would* get a job. I *might* make it through the next eight days.

And I wandered down to a crest just below the damn, feeling newly invigorated, and what I saw next just blew my 6.0 beer-addled mind.

I had come to look for America, but I had landed in Southeast Asia.

Because there in the shallows, on the banks of the Walnut, a contingent of least a dozen Vietnamese Refugees (at the time known as *Boat People*) had set up camp.

And they were amazing to watch.

They ranged in age from seven to seventy. The men and boys were fishing with drop lines with the tiniest hooks I had ever seen, catching *not* Big Catfish and Carp, but little minnows and other bait fish.

The women were scraping lichen off the bottoms of rocks and scouring the pebbles for snails and crawfish.

And *all* this stuff went into one big gun-metal pot, which sat simmering over a small fire, at the top of which floated several fish heads.

I approached to within a few feet of that pot and the ancient Vietnamese woman who was tending it smiled up at me and said, in fractured but legible English...

"You like?"

And I said, "Yes."

And she said, "You want?"

And I said, "Maybe later."

The girls were a few yards downstream, washing clothing in the calmer water, literally beating them with rocks.

It was frigging fascinating.

I had heard about these Boat People from Townies. How they were brought over just recently, sponsored by various church groups. How there were Vietnamese and maybe Cambodians. How there was some friction between they and the locals.

But I didn't see any of that at Tunnel Mill Dam.

There were local teenagers partying at the picnic tables. There were local anglers, in their waders, with big 10' fishing poles going for the "big ones." There were the Vietnamese or Cambodians (or both) quietly, doggedly going about their business.

And there was me, sitting on my duffel bag, my ersatz camping permit in hand, thinking after what these people have been through, I can sure as hell make it another eight days.

It was Springtime In Kansas. The wind was rustling through the pecan trees and the oak trees and that white water verily thundered over that low, stone dam.

Ar-KAN-*SAW*, Ar-*KANSAS*.

Kansans, Oklahomans.

Vietnamese, Cambodians.

Imaginary lines, I thought. Exaggerated boundaries.

And that fish-head stew was starting to look pretty damn good to me.

CHAPTER 6

DISHES FIRST. FORKS SECOND.

Day Three of my ten day quest to look for America found me awakening atop a picnic table at Tunnel Mill Dam on the Southwest side of Winfield. My Captain's Log indicated I had been on the road for 50 hours and had traveled a disappointing 130 miles…maybe.

I had 21 bucks left, and had been warned *twice* by the W.P.D. that I had better make some changes in my life or I was flirting with a vagrancy charge. Other than that the cops were pretty nice.

As I awoke to the roar of the water over the damn and the cheerful chirping of birds in the pecan, oak and pine trees, I stirred the ashes in the small fire that myself and the Boat People had made the night before and it flamed to life.

It was early, just past dawn, and the Boat People and teenagers and anglers from the day before were all gone. And I knew if I was going to make it through the next seven days I would need more money. I would have to get a job.

I already *had* two jobs, but they were both at Southwestern College (which was closed for Spring Break) and they did me little good now. I needed something that would pay daily, like today's temp employers.

I also, as always, needed a place to stay. Tunnel Mill was fine for a night, but even though it was April in Kansas it wasn't even close to warm at night. So—a job and a room—and surprisingly it took about 20 minutes to secure one of those.

I got the job first. Walking North on Main Street, I passed a little "diner" called The Honey Tree. Outside, the street was packed with farm trucks and pick ups. Inside it was also packed, mostly farmers and roustabouts. Men in flannel and denim and skin like dried leather.

And a sign in the window said HELP WANTED.

I walked to the counter and took the place in. The joint was filled with smoke and the aroma of fresh-brewed coffee and sizzling bacon. My stomach did flips because I had not eaten in almost two days. And, folks, this place was *a-hopping.*

Two harried, pink-aproned waitresses with paper hats scurried about, picking up and dropping plates, emptying ashtrays and refilling coffee and plastic glasses of iced tea, sweetened only, please. The short-order cook in the back was banging that pick-up bell in the service window every ten seconds.

At each table was a Mini-Juke Box that patrons could flip through and select their own private breakfast music. Somebody must have really liked Waylon and Willie, because *Mamas Don't Let Your Babies Grow Up To Be Cowboys* played over and over again.

And the checkout lady was banging and fingering that old wood and brass cash register like she was playing a Ragtime Piano.

"It'll be a minute," she said to me, not looking up from her pecking and ticket stabbing.

"I'm looking for a job," I said.

Without, again, looking up, she said

"When can you start?"

And I said, "Now."

Here was the deal: The Honey Tree was open from 5:30 A.M. until 2:00 P.M., six days a week. And I was the new dishwasher. It paid $1.50 per hour, plus all the eggs and chicken fried steak and biscuits and gravy I could eat. And yes, she would pay me every day after my shift. They would "try me out" right then.

Within seconds I was handed a white, thick, dirty apron and was whisked into the cramped kitchen where the short-order cook was in such a frenzied flip and stir and ladle and bell-ringing mode he didn't even notice me at first.

His name was Frank, about 60, rail-thin, unshaven, heavily-tattooed and quick as a rattlesnake. And being dressed in white from cap to shoes he was simply covered in grease and gravy stains.

When he wasn't wielding that spatula like a Ninja Chef he was lighting a no-filter Lucky Strike cigarette and swigging from a 40 oz. oil can of Colt .45 Malt Liquor.

This man had it down.

Smoke, drink, flip, stir, ladle, serve-up, ring, drink. Smoke, drink, flip, stir, ladle, serve-up, ring, drink. It was this incredible, unchoreographed ballet of skill, slobbery and vice.

After a few moments of watching Frank do his thing, I realized just what I had gotten into. It had to be over 100 degrees in there. A steaming, stinking 100 degrees. And a veritable mountain of filthy dishes, cups, glasses, flatware, pots and pans awaited me, piled high in teetering towers of cast iron and porcelain. And before I could even get the water hot Frank was yelling

"DISHES FIRST, *ASSHOLE*! DISHES FIRST! "

So I did the dishes first.

But I couldn't do them fast enough to keep up with the big, gray plastic bussing bins filled with kitchenware and cigarette butts and concrete egg yolks that the two waitresses would drop at my feet every five minutes.

Two hours later, after the breakfast rush, I had a chance to catch up, and this I did. "I'll show that bastard Frank," I thought.

When he took his break, sitting on a milk crate by the open back door, smoking his Lucky and sucking on his fourth Colt .45 Malt Liquor, I stood there, proud as a peacock, before a disaster of a kitchen I had scrubbed and washed and dried and stacked until it looked *fantastic*.

One of the waitresses, Angela, in her 30s, and looking worn out from the morning's craziness, her blonde hair plastered to her forehead, peeked in and said

"Holy Shit! Come look at this!"

And the check-out lady and the other waitress peeked in.

"Damn," the check-out lady said. And I knew I had passed the audition.

I waited for Frank to respond to this small miracle, to ascertain and recognize my value to this operation. To *realize* I had turned his shithole of a kitchen into a place that with just a little bit of bribery *might* pass a Board of Health Inspection.

But *this* is what I got:

"Dishes first, Asshole," Frank said. "Forks second."

After the lunch rush I had this place figured out down cold. It was not rocket science. It was dishes and dirt and a crusty old bastard. But I had to admire him in some odd way, and *this is why:*

Just like the classic episode of *W.K.R.P. In Cincinnati* (where Dr. Johnny Fever gets faster as he gets drunker) that was Frank! The more Colt .45 oil cans that man chugged down, the more efficient he became.

The man was a certifiable artist at the grill and deep fryer. And even though he *also* became a more irascible, insufferable son-of-a-bitch as the fortified beer went down…

"Damn College Boy! Look at you NOW, College Boy!"

…I *still* knew talent when I saw it.

Turns out that ol' crotchety prick spent most of his Pre-Honey Tree career in the Navy as a cook. So, I figured cooking for a tiny diner on Main Street, Winfield, KS, was a lead-pipe-cinch compared to cooking for 1000 old tars on a battleship somewhere in the Adriatic.

I'd like to tell you that over the next few days Frank and I became friends and that he really was a great guy. But I can't do that because not *one time* have I lied during this tale and I am not going to start now. I will simply use the phrase my Father taught me oh-so-well.

"Once a prick. Always a prick."

I left The Honey Tree six hours later and nine bucks richer than when I walked in that morning. And things were looking up.

Just a few blocks further North on Main was a two story, white brick building called The Callison Hotel and much like the St. Elmo Hotel in Burden, it resembled a "hotel" in name only.

It was two floors, old wood and plaster and few rooms with furniture that looked as if it was all picked up from a garage sale. Decor from the 40s, 50s and 60s was well represented there but not in any unified fashion.

But it was a room with a bath down the hall. And it was five dollars a night (*Must Be Payable In Cash Daily At 12:00 P.M.*) And for the first time in three days I could put down that heavy frigging duffel bag, take a bath, wash the road and wood smoke and the kitchen grease from myself and change clothes in private.

It was almost 3 P.M. now, and, considering my dire financial state of earlier that day, I was flush. And I deserved a break. Just a little diversion for myself after so many long hard crazy hours on the road.

As Elmer Fudd would say, I needed some *west and wewaxation*.

So, I decided to go to a bar.

And here is something interesting:

For a town that only served 3.2 beer they had a buttload of places to sell it in. There was *Joe's City Cigar Store*,

The Little Casino, The Pub, Buck and Jean's, The Lantern, The Cellar, T.C.'S Hickory Pub, and the *L.B.J.* (which stood not for the 36th President of the United States but for *Lyle's Beer Joint.*)

And there were three or four others I cannot recall.

But I *do* recall the ones mentioned above, all eight of them. And before that afternoon and night was over, I hit every damn one of them.

CHAPTER 7

THE BEE GEES SUCK AND WILL ALWAYS SUCK

Day Four of my ten day spate of homelessness found me back in Winfield with a tiny, Five-Buck-A-Night room at the Callison Hotel, a job washing dishes at the Honey Tree Diner, and almost 30 dollars in the front right pocket of my 501s.

As I mentioned earlier, for a town that only sold 3.2. beer, Winfield had a ton of places to drink it in. And I was going to try to hit all of them, for no other reason than my look for America tour had left me very bored and very thirsty.

I started at *The Pub,* the kinda' "bad boy" hang out in town. It was the preferred watering hole of The Delts, of which I was a member, and of perhaps the unpolite side of Winfield Society. Bikers, rednecks, roustabouts. I once saw a guy on a motorcycle come in the back door, do a burn out on the dance floor and head out the front door.

The bartender didn't even look up.

How cool was that?

But *The Pub* was more prone to nighttime debauchery, for those who avoided the sun, and being late afternoon the place was dead. But they did have a great jukebox, and

I spent a few quarters listening to *ZZ Top, Jethro Tull, Led Zeppelin, Aerosmith* and *Molly Hatchet.*

There was no disco on that jukebox, and for that I was grateful. Because (and I will touch upon this later) disco about damn near ruined my entire "college experience."

I left *The Pub* and walked just a few doors down to *The Little Casino.* And it *was* little: a 12 foot bar, four tables, a pool table and a long, sawdust covered shuffle-board table.

The clientele here was hard to describe. I could say they were "men of leisure" (meaning 11:00 A.M. drunks) but that would be a bit unfair. This crew of mainly "cowboy" types just were on a different schedule then most. The jukebox there was almost entirely country music and golden oldies.

And my Winfield City Pub Crawl (before we called them Pub Crawls) continued on from there.

I worked my way North on the West Side of Main Street, and stopped in *The L.B.J.* This was *Lyle's Beer Joint* and if you want to talk about truth in advertising, *The L.B.J.* was all it professed to be--a beer Joint. Presumably run by Lyle. It had all the charm and atmosphere of a dry cleaners.

From there I went farther North and crossed over Main Street to *Buck And Jean's* (which was also a Beer Joint, presumably run by Buck and/or Jean.) I didn't find out *who* exactly because I didn't stay long. The place was really just a step up from *The Little Casino*, but a short step.

Working my way back South on Main, I took a slight jag on 9th and stopped in at *The Lantern.* Why this place was called *The Lantern*, I have no idea, because it was dark as hell inside all the time. And I didn't stay there long either. There were three reasons for these short stays:

1. At all these places thus far I was still "the kid." I had barely turned 18 and the patrons of these taverns were older and a bit stoic, meaning the moment I walked into any of these places I was greeted with looks of "*Who the hell is this now?*" or "*Well, what do we have here?*"

2. There is only so much you can do with 3.2. beer. You can put tomato juice in it. You could put salt and pepper in it. You could doctor it with lemons and olive juice and limes, but it will always still taste like Rocky Mountain Piss Water.

3. The only place in town where I knew I *might* find people my age was *JOE'S,* and they were not open yet.

I had hit five of Winfield's Public Houses and was not even buzzed. But I still really should have eaten something. I didn't because the three-pound serving of biscuits and gravy I had eaten at the Honey Tree around 2:00 was laying in my stomach like a sack of wet cement.

Joe's City Cigar Store (right across the street from *The Pub)* was definitely the Default Tap Room for the students at Southwestern, St. John's University and Cowley County Community College. This was my ilk.

It was a *lonnnnnng* place, with a solid wood bar, pinball machines and dart boards. Toward the back were two, huge snooker tables, and two regular pool tables, bar-sized.

Behind the bar was an ancient Well's Fargo safe that stood about five feet tall. And if you and your pals could move it, you could drink free for the rest of the night. I saw many a jock herniate in that attempt. But I never saw anyone budge the damn thing.

They even had a mounted Jack-O-Lope. And being from Long Island I will admit the first time I saw it, I actually pondered whether or not it was real for a few seconds.

Joe Steiner, owner and lead barkeep, was a tall, thin, amicable man, who always seemed to be wearing a collared white shirt and a white apron. He set aside Wednesday and Friday nights mainly for the college crowd, with discounts and live music and D.J.s.

He also offered up a thing called The Fish Bowl. This was about 36 ounces of beer in a big-ass glass. And he frosted these mugs so thoroughly that you couldn't even touch them for a few minutes without the risk of frostbite. This was 3 bucks.

Lord, take me back.

So, Wednesdays and Fridays being a mix of neophyte drinkers, cheap beer and testosterone, things could get a bit rowdy. There was usually a tussle or two, resulting in the participants being banned for about a week.

That might not sound like much, but it was a big hit to the social calendar of a lot of kids. After a week, Joe, would let you back in, but *only* if you also apologized. Which, of course I did on several occasions.

But all in all it was just good times and great fun, *until* Joe, always aware of current trends, opened up a back room and on the ceiling *he hung a disco ball.*

W.T.F.?

I'M 18! I COME FROM WORLD OF ROCK AND ROLL!

SIXTIES AND SEVENTIES ROCK AND ROLL!
ARGUABLY THE BEST DAMN ROCK AND ROLL EVER!
SEX! DRUGS! ROCK AND ROLL!

I knew I was in Kansas and I would have to take a little dose of Country Music with my Rock & Roll, but Disco went light years beyond the pale.

And on those two college nights a week, Broc Swedenborg and Stretch Singleton would host and set up an ear-drum shattering D.J. Booth with strobes and blinkers and that *damn disco ball* and pollute the air with the frigging Bee Gees.

The shrieking…

…nasal…

…gold-lame clad…

…platformed-shoed…

…gold-chain festooned…

…chest hair preening…

…warbling…

…bat-wing blow-dried…

…falsetto yodeling…

…assassins of good music everywhere.

THE TOP FORTY WAS INFECTED WITH DISCO FROM ALL THE ONE-HIT WONDER DISCO PERPETRATORS!

Nobody *ever* proclaimed *"SEX! DRUGS! K.C. AND THE SUNSHINE BAND!"*

But I digress…still ruing the day disco arrived at *Joe's City Cigar Store.* That night (and I thank the gods of good music everywhere) the college kids were on spring break and

Joe had suspended disco night, and at 7:00 P.M. I walked inside *Joe's City Cigar Store* and the place was packed.

The pool balls were clacking.

The darts were flying.

The Fish Bowls were dripping ice.

And the jukebox was playing *Dust In The Wind*. *Ahhhhh, Ahhhhh, Kansas!*

Those boys could rock. Hell, they invented a new form of rock.

It would be a good night, I thought. Good music. Cheap beer. Lots of local girls hanging about. All was right with the world.

But six hours later I was sitting outside the jail in Arkansas City, wondering just how the hell I got there.

CHAPTER 8

BLONDIE

Winfield, KS. April 1978. Joe's City Cigar Store. 9:00 P.M.

After spending the night before sleeping on a picnic table in Tunnel Mill Park, I had spent this day getting a job washing dishes at the Honey Tree Cafe, securing a room at the Callison Hotel, and (using my new found wealth—almost 30 bucks in the front right pocket of my 501s) I did as much bar-hopping as one could hop in the Winfield, KS of that year.

After short visits to *The Pub, The Little Casino Club, L.B.J.'s, Buck and Jeans* and *The Lantern*, I settled in at *Joe's City Cigar Store*, the preferred public house of both locals and college kids, and was reveling in the fact it was not Disco Night. Jim Stinson was there, playing *Marshall Tucker* on the Juke Box, over and over and over again. And that suited me just frigging fine.

The Drennan Boys were there (Dougie and Darryl) big-toothed smiling linemen from Southwestern College, who also lived in town. And the largest Drennan, Dave, was home on his Spring Break from Southwest Missouri State.

Big Lou Mignone, a Long Island Native like myself, sat on his usual stool (no one else would dare sit there) in his shorts, even though it was a cool 44 degrees out. Lou would wear his shorts in a blizzard, so that was nothing new.

Southern Rock and *B.T.O* and *Aerosmith* blared. Snooker balls whizzed and clacked. The Playboy pinball machine chimed and buzzed. Joe Steiner pulled frosted fish bowls from his freezer and the beer foam oozed like sweet meringue onto the bar top.

After 63 straight hours of lunacy I had landed some-place familiar.

It had a been a long day but a good day compared to last two, and I sat at the bar by myself and took time to reflect on how I would get through the next seven days until they opened the dorms back up and I could resume my education, such as it was.

Any thoughts I had about resuming my hitch-hiking *Look for America* adventure had lost their appeal. But I had collected some fantastic, sometimes terrifying experiences. And I had collected so many stories that someday I might tell to someone. Somewhere. Somehow.

Hell, I might even write them down.

The main difference between this night and the pre-vious two were that there was no mystery involved. There would be no more surprises. I *knew* what I was doing now (staying out of trouble) what I would be doing later (crashing at the Callison) and what I would be doing tomorrow morning at 5:30 A.M. (slapping on my apron at The Honey Tree.)

This cycle would hopefully repeat itself until next Monday. And I had resigned myself, happily, wearily--to *normalcy.* And just as you *might* think this protracted tale is over, at the time, so did I.

But I could not have been more wrong.

Because at about 9:45 P.M. a long, cool woman in tight jeans, cowboy boots, a white cotton shirt and a Haliburton baseball cap came up to me, tapped me on the shoulder and said

"Can I take you home?"

Let's back up here a bit.

I believe I have already mentioned earlier my complete ineptitude when it comes to women of any kind. So, not only had I never, *ever* had to field such a proposal before, I was also clueless as to how to frame a response.

But in the three seconds after that *long cool woman* said, "Can I take you home?" my synapses were firing off a million questions in my head:

DID YOU JUST SAY WHAT I THINK YOU SAID? WHO ARE YOU? DO YOU KNOW ME? DO I KNOW YOU? HAVE WE MET BEFORE? IF SO, WHERE? WHOSE "HOME" ARE WE TALKING ABOUT HERE? MY "HOME?" YOU'RE "HOME?" IS THIS A JOKE? WHO PUT YOU UP TO THIS? DID DRENNAN PUT YOU UP TO THIS? IF SO— WHICH DAMN DRENNAN?! DID STINSON PUT YOU UP TO THIS, THE BASTARD!? NO WAY I'M FALLING FOR THIS CRAP. OR IS IT CRAP? CHRIST—SAY SOMETHING, DELANEY!

The woman stood there patiently, a slight, cryptic smile on her face, her blue eyes clear and her expression without guile or any hint of deceit. She popped a hip in what I assumed was some small amount of impatience and took off her hat. And when she did, about 14" of straight blonde, lustrous hair draped her shoulders.

And what I said to her will confirm in your minds that when I say I have absolutely not a scintilla of instinct when it comes to women I was not lying. Because what I said was

"Maybe later."

And she nodded slightly and went back to where she came from, which was a booth way down deep in the bar by the snooker tables, at least 50 feet away, where she and three of what I assumed were her girlfriends were gathered.

And I sat there thinking: *this was some kind of silly bet that this woman either won or lost,* and I wasn't going to pay it any more mind. And I just nursed my Fish Bowl and put a little tomato juice in it and played a few *Warren Zevon* songs and forgot about the whole thing until at 11:45 P.M. Joe called LAST CALL! and a few seconds later that blonde woman tapped me on the shoulder again and said

"You ready?"

And I said…

"Yes."

Her name was Teresa. And she worked for Haliburton Oil as a roustabout. A pretty tough gig for a woman at the time. She had a banged up Ford Ranger pick-up and in the bed were her big pipe wrenches, her hard hat and her greasy coveralls.

She was an Ark City Girl and that was new to me, because the way she said "I'm an Ark City Girl" implied there was some tangible difference between a Winfield Girl or a Southwestern Girl and, indeed, an Ark City Girl. There wasn't any difference to me, however, because they all seemed to have the same working parts and the same formidable air of unconquerability that had always confounded me.

I was, frankly, still stunned something such as this was actually happening to me as we headed South on 77, *into* Ark City, *through* Ark City and then *out* of Ark City.

Next thing I knew I was back in Oklahoma.

"I thought you lived in Ark City," I said.

And she said, "I do. But I'm not done yet."

A few miles later, on the East Side of Highway 77, she pulled into the gravel parking lot loaded with pick up trucks. I am still not sure where exactly this was. But it was not the roadhouse I had stopped at the day before.

It was a steel Quonset Hut with a big metal door and two windows, both of which displayed neon Bud Light signs. Before we even got out of the car you could feel the bass from some honky tonk redneck rendition pulsing through the air.

Well, I thought, *It's just a bar.* I had been in a lot of bars that day. Townie Bars, Cowboy Bars, College Bars, Old Man Bars. How could one more hurt? And how could this place be any different?

Well, I'll tell you how.

This was *not* a Drugstore Cowboy Joint.

This was a *REAL* Cowboy Joint.

Big Buckles. Shit-Covered Boots. Sweaty, stained felt and straw-woven Cowboy Hats. Faded and incredibly tight, painted on jeans. Plaid, collared shirts and Bolo ties. Women in tank tops and shirts tied at the waist.

It was raucous, dirty, smoky, beer stinking…and *loud*.

When we entered the patrons were in the final choruses of *Jerry Jeff Walker's Redneck Mother*. And they sang it loudly and proudly:

SO WELL, SO WELL, SO GODDAMN WELL

David Allan Coe followed immediately. And they sang that, too:

IF THAT AIN'T COUNTRY, I'LL KISS YOUR ASS.

But they did not sing KISS. They sang KICK. And I do believe they meant it. And then another *David Allan Coe* song came on that I do not believe ever actually made commercial airplay in these United States. But it was on the juke box. It was about two women:

FINGER F----ING SALLY
and P------Y EATING PAM

And I really should not go into the particulars of that little ditty at this time, or, hell, any *other* time for that matter.

At this point my and Teresa's idea of what exactly *Can I take you home?* meant were diverging on many fronts. But I was willing to explore this new risk in lieu of possible reward.

And it was *then* I noticed two more things about this place that set it apart from all the places I had been to thus far in the state of Kansas.

1. They sold LIQUOR, not just 3.2. beer. And it was *a-flowin'*.

2. Every man-jack in that joint, and half the women, were packin' heat.

And I mean guns in holsters on hips.

Thank you, Teresa Darling, for taking me to a Quonset Hut in Northern Oklahoma at 1:00 A.M. where the evening's entertainment includes Dolly Parton, Pabst Blue Ribbon, Patron Tequila and pistols.

CHAPTER 9

NO ONE HERE GETS OUT ALIVE

So, my new friend (That long, cool blonde named Teresa. That Ark City Girl. That woman who walked up to me at *Joe's City Cigar Store* in Winfield, KS, and actually said, "Can I take you home?") INSTEAD took me a Quonset Hut Honky Tonk Redneck Roadhouse somewhere just South of the Kansas-Oklahoma line.

And the joint was jumpin'. It was 1:30 A.M. now, and, whereas over the line in Kansas the bars were all closed, these lunatics were just getting started.

It had everything a New Yorker like me would think a Cowboy Bar ought to have:

~*George Jones, Waylon Jennings, Tanya Tucker* and *Johnny Cash* on the juke box with a bass so heavy it rattled your fillings? CHECK!

~A full service bar with shots of rye and mezcal and cheap beer chasers consumed at alarming rates? CHECK!

~Pointy-Toed Armadillo "shit-kicker" boots, sported by broad-shouldered, thin-waisted Goat Ropers dancing with their thumbs hooked into their belt loops? CHECK!

~Bra-less Women in too-tight jeans and halter tops, two-stepping on the bar. HELL YES CHECK!

~Firearms? CHECK!

Yes, I checked off firearms because almost all of the guys and some of the girls had handguns on their hips in holsters. Black guns, gray guns, silver guns, snub-nosed guns, long barrel guns, pearl handles, oak handles, walnut handles, Army .45s, .22s and .38 Specials.

"Christ," I said to Teresa, "Everyone's got a gun!"

And she said, "Ah, shoot! I left mine in the car."

We got alcohol, *David Allan Coe* and ammunition, folks! What could possibly go wrong?

My "date," such as she was *thus far*, seemed to know everyone in the place and took to introducing me to many of them by saying

"Howdy, this is my friend…um…*what's* your name again?"

And I would say "Doug," but little more, because I had already experienced the effect that a New York Accent heard in any Kansas or Oklahoma bar had on people.

It was never anything good. And I was always outnumbered.

At *Joe's City Cigar Store*, I could hold my own because I *knew* many of those folks, and my standard, though always-morphing response to inevitable the *Noo Yawk* insults was:

"Ah, yes, Kansas—where the men are men and the women are men and the sheep are nervous."

And that usually shut them up. But there was *no way* I was gonna' drop that line in a bar where there was Colt .45 Beer *and* Colt .45 Revolvers.

And when Theresa's friends would ask me "Where ya'll from?" (*as if there were two of me*) I'd say "Eastern Kansas" and that seemed to work.

I had really hoped that when Teresa first approached me in that bar so many miles away, the subsequent experience would be more carnal then terrifying, but she seemed to have her own way of going about things and I figured there would be a payoff at the end.

In the meantime, I just watched her play pool (that was fun), sipped my Buck Horn beer and kept my Yankee Trap verily shut.

And then, *it hit me…*

I had an epiphany of sorts.

Though it seemed like weeks, I had started out this journey days ago (alone, pissed off, heartbroken and broke) in the hope of *Looking for America*. And though, in miles, my travels might have been minimal, in experiencing the people and places of Southeast Kansas and Northeast Oklahoma I had traversed parsecs.

And sitting there at this No Name Roadhouse, I realized I was also a *traveler in time*.

Because, with the exception of the modern convenience of electricity, this place is *exactly* what some lonesome stranger could have walked into 100 years earlier. I just as well could have been in:

DODGE CITY, KANSAS. APRIL 1878.
THE LONG BRANCH SALOON
100 years earlier…

I enter the Long Branch Saloon, weary from the road. And I use my cowboy hat to knock the dust off my calf-skin poncho. The fiddle player is wheedling out *Turkey in the Straw*, accompanied by a badly-tuned piano.

The saloon girls are dancing and the gamblers are Bucking the Tiger.

The cowboys, fresh in from their long drive up from Amarillo, are A-WHOOPIN' and A-HOLLERIN' and blowing holes in the ceiling with their Navy Colt Revolvers.

The air is filled with blue gunsmoke and the spittoons *pa-TING* as the spurs jingle and jangle. It is a hot time in the old town tonight. And I wrap my knuckles on the bar and say "Whiskey, barkeep. And leave the bottle." And I pull the cork out with my teeth and spit it up in the air.

And a saloon girl (we will call her Teresa) sidles up to me and says

"Hello, handsome stranger. New in these here parts?"

And *that* is about as far as my epiphany got. Because back in 1978 the bartender was waving the phone over his head and yelling

"Teresa! You got a phone call!"

And Teresa took that call. And she hung up. And she headed for the door, grabbing me by the arm on her way out and said

"We gotta' go! Like NOW!"

So, I am thinking what you are thinking:

Teresa is *married*. Or Teresa has a gun-totin', tobacco-chewing boyfriend who is on his way down here right now loaded for bear and unsuspecting Long Islanders.

It was after 2:00 A.M.

And where we were heading, Teresa wasn't saying.

But we spun out of that parking lot in that little old

pick-up putting up a roiling cloud of dust in the air and sending gravel plinking off that metal building like machine gun bullets.

Apparently, this night was not yet over.

And looking back on the hasty exit I only wish to hell that instead of saying to me "We gotta' go! Like *NOW*!" that Teresa would have said

"Time to get the hell out of Dodge."

CHAPTER TEN

ARE THOSE HAND-CUFFS,
OR ARE YOU JUST HAPPY TO SEE ME?

Somewhere In Northern Oklahoma, 2:10 A.M., April 1978

So as my unexpected date, Ark City Teresa, that lanky blonde tornado, peeled out of the Okie Roadhouse parking lot, I hung onto the dashboard and was hopeful she was going to make good on her request to "take me home." And when she pointed her battered little pick'em'up back North toward Ark City, that did seem to be the case.

And I said, "Are you *really* taking me home now?"

And she said, "Lord knows, I'm trying."

I took her haste (doing almost 80 in a 55) as a sign she was anxious to get to the fun stuff as I was. But, and you should *know* or at least surmise from previous chapters, that is not exactly what happened next. I mean, the way things had been going, how could this possibly go right?

Instead of taking me to some cozy, little bachelorette love nest somewhere in A.C., she took me to a far less inviting little place called jail. She pulled into the police station parking lot, left the engine running, hopped out and said, "I'll be right back."

Normally, this is something that might have upset me, but in the *Mr. Toad's Wild Ride* that had been my existence since my journey started, I had grown quite accustomed to the residents of Southern Kansas and Northern Oklahoma being certifiably fucking insane.

So why should Teresa be any different?

Forty-five minutes later, a bit after 3:00 A.M., Teresa exited the front door of the police station with one cop and one shirtless, Snaggy-Do type young man in handcuffs. You have seen this guy.

This is the guy with the chipped tooth who gets arrested twice a week outside his trash strewn single-wide trailer on *COPS!* for setting the neighbor's cats on fire. This is the guy they pick up twice a week because they just know he did it.

No shirt, half a beard, matted long hair, too many tattoos and sweatpants.

The cop, who seemed to know Teresa well, unlocked the handcuffs and set his prisoner free, apparently into her custody. As Snaggy-Do and Blondie headed toward the truck, I heard the cop say, "I swear to God, Teresa, next time he's going to *real* jail."

Teresa's pick'em'up, of course, had no back seat. And I did not give a damn what was going to happen next except for the fact that I was not gonna' ride bitch. I got out and opened the door for Snaggy-Do.

He said nothing, slid inside, and stared dead ahead.

And that is when my fair Teresa unloaded on his redneck ass but good.

"You ignorant dumbass *muthafucker*!" Teresa explained. "I get ONE DAMN NIGHT OFF A WEEK and here I am bailing your sorry ass out of jail--AGAIN! And in case you haven't noticed, I am not alone!"

At this point it seemed that Snaggy-Do actually noticed I was sitting there.

"Hey," he said.

And I said, "Hey."

And he said, "Got any beer?"

Teresa's dressing down went on for quite a while as we drove through the darkened streets of Ark City and, yes, *across the tracks* into a fairly blighted neighborhood of crappy trailers and shotgun shacks.

Snaggy-Do was Teresa's bother. He was the one who called that Roadhouse Bar from jail. And that kicked off a few questions in my head:

~You get one phone call after your arrest for *whatever* and you *call the bar*?

~Why were you in jail?

~It's down to 38 degrees. *Where* is your damn shirt?!?

I didn't actually ASK any of those questions because frankly, I didn't want to know the answers. Outside of Snaggy-Do's trailer, Teresa skidded up on the grass, threw open her door and said

"Get the hell out."

And Snaggy-Do said, "Can't."

And Teresa said, "Bull*SHIT*, you can't! GET OUT!"

And Snaggy-Do said those two magical words that practically cemented the fact I was not going to lie in Teresa's lovin' arms that night.

And those two magical words were:

"Restraining Order."

Snaggy-Do was banned from his own domicile by legal writ.

Teresa sighed the saddest damn *sigh*. She looked at me with those big, powder blue eyes and I could tell she was just as disappointed as I was.

So off to her house we went. Teresa and Doug *plus one*.

And this third wheel couldn't have been squeakier. When we pulled into Teresa's driveway, Snaggy-Do said

"Take me down to Oklahoma, Bitch. Bars ain't closed yet."

And Teresa took an oil-covered work boot out of the back of the pick'em'up and proceeded to beat her brother up the driveway, across the porch and into the house with it. He tried to shuck and jive out of the way, but she did not miss his head once.

She then got back in the driver's seat and said

"'Spose you wouldn't care to come inside?"

And I said, "You 'spose correctly."

So that was that. Game over, Doug Delaney. The Luck of the Irish has once again ditched you in your hour of need. And then Teresa said

"How about YOU take ME home?"

And there it was.

I did not have a home but had paid for a room at the Callison Hotel and it had been sitting there empty since 2:00 P.M. the day before.

And here I say unto you again, hope sprang eternal.

It was almost 4:00 A.M. when we arrived 14 miles to the North at the Callison Hotel on Main Street in Winfield,

KS. Teresa parked the little truck in the diagonal space right by the front glass door entrance and we sat there for quite a while in numbed silence.

Finally, the eagle had landed.

When I first met Teresa at *Joe's City Cigar Store* nine hours earlier the whole encounter seemed more of a "hook up" than anything else. But I had grown to really like her and respect her for how tough she was. And now I could see she was dealing with a lot more crap than just working in an oil field 17 hours a day.

And, tough as she was, she seemed suddenly vulnerable…suddenly very sad and in need of a friend more than a one-night-stand.

Don't you think that should have stopped me from pursuing the matter any further?

Don't you think some chivalric sense of human decency should have prevailed here?

Don't you? Huh??

Hell, no.

So we headed to the big front glass doors of the Callison Hotel, arms around each other's waists, and giggling with anticipation. And of course them doors were locked up tighter than a clam's ass.

WHAT HOTEL LOCKS IT'S DOORS!

I pounded for at least five minutes on the doors to no avail.

Teresa, bless her heart, just laughed with resignation.

This eagle had landed in a pile of crap.

This could only mean one thing: breakfast.

I had to be at work anyway in about an hour, so we walked down to the Honey Tree Café and sat on the park bench outside until Frank (the short-order cook from hell) arrived with a bag of Colt. 45 oil cans under his arm, unlocked the doors and in we went.

I donned my apron and Teresa said I looked "cute" and the rest of the wait staff (Angie and Carmen) arrived and well, of course, they *knew* Teresa and settled in over gossip and fresh coffee. And Carmen said

"Looks like you hooked a live one, Noo Yawk."

And back in that inferno of a kitchen, while Frank fired up that big black gas behemoth of a stove, he leaned into me (he was not quite yet drunk) and said, somehow derisively

"Didn't know you had it in 'ya, College Boy."

And I, having now been up for at least 27 hours straight, told Frank to kindly go fuck himself.

CHAPTER 11

I'M JUST A HUNKA HUNKA BURNIN' LOVE

I will tell you now this tale does not end nicely. How could it? As you have read thus far the entire adventure has been an unmitigated disaster, a train-wreck of an excursion that started out with high hopes and ignorant bliss, and ended in abject confusion and misery.

I had been up for 35 hours straight when my shift washing dishes at the Honey Tree ended and all I wanted to do was get to my crappy, little room at the Callison Hotel and dive face first into those onion-skin thin sheets and slip into a much-needed coma.

Teresa, my long cool Ark City blonde "date" from the night before, had headed back into the oil fields to start her shift about six hours earlier. I would not see her again for quite a while. But I would see her again, and that was not such a bad thing.

I was so damn tired the events of the last four days didn't even seem real. The break up...Klos's term paper... The Winfield Cops...the Dynamite Twins...the Burden Ball-Busters...that Howling Lunatic, Truman...sleeping on the road...The Bruner Brothers...Marlboro Man and that Gorgeous Cowgirl...the vacant rolling highways and the

apocalyptic thunderstorms…the Winfield Cops again…
the Boat People…sleeping down at the river…the Honey
Tree and that Idiot-Savant short order cook, Frank…and
then last night: The Winfield Pub Crawl, the gun-toting
Oklahoma Cowboys, the Ark City Police Station and finally
being locked out of the Callison Hotel.

Walking North on Main Street I decided there and
then that until my dorm opened up in about three days
I would do nothing. I would wash the damn dishes, collect
my $1.50 an hour, and sit in my room, lamenting my 18
year old life.

I would sit in that room and write letters. I would write
Nancy Mathews volumes, inquiring as to why she actually
dumped me the day before Spring Break, telling her why it
wasn't such a good move on her part. I would write Chris
Klos (Kick'n K.C.) and apologize for promising him an A
term paper and maybe not giving it my best effort. I would
write my friend Laurel back in New York and not tell her a
damn thing about these last few days. I would lay low, and
not put myself in the path of any more insanity. This was
the plan.

And, of course, none of that actually happened.

Because from over a block away I spied something out
on the sidewalk in front of the Callison Hotel that was
all-too-familiar. It was my green army duffel bag, atop of
which sat my poor excuse for a cowboy hat.

What…the…fuck?

I grabbed my bag and my hat and went inside and con-
fronted the old lady who ran this joint and inquired, in
different words, "What…the…fuck?"

And the upshot was that I had been evicted, for cause. What happened was this:

My deal with the Callison Hotel was to pay my $5.00 a night fee before noon on a daily basis. But at noon that day I was up to my elbows in greasy pots and pans and bitching Frank at the Honey Tree. I informed the old lady that had I *not* been locked out of the hotel the night before I would have gladly left the damn five bucks in my room.

She was not swayed.

"I lock the doors at 11:00" she said. "Anyone not in by then has no business staying here."

And that was that: The Wisdom and Intractability of Age versus the apparent Delinquency of My Youth. I was persona-non-grata at the Callison Hotel.

The road goes on forever, People, and the party never ends.

But it *had to end!* Not only was I sleep walking but in my haste to go to bed I had forgotten to eat my complimentary, heart-clogging three pounds of biscuits and gravy at The Honey Tree. And my stomach was flipping like an epileptic flounder.

It was then I decided (for the first time in my life) to pretty much break the law. I'm not sure if it was a "law" as defined by Kansas Statute but it was definitely a "law" at Southwestern College. I would walk the three miles to my dormitory, Reid Hall, pray the lobby doors were unlocked, and just sneak back into my room.

I justified this by telling myself, *hell, my parents paid for this damn room*—might as well use it.

On the way to campus I stopped by Wheeler's I.G.A. and picked up two frozen pizzas. When I got to campus the place was crawling with maintenance vans doing whatever it is they do to the dorm rooms while the students were away. The presence of staff was unsettling but the good news was that every dorm had their main entrance doors chocked wide open.

And I just slipped right in, hustled to Second Floor East and I was home. I needed a shower and I needed to eat but one of the oddities of Reid Hall was that every circular floor shared a communal bathroom and also the only stove in the place was in the third floor lounge.

And I could not risk that kind of exposure.

I could see out my window that a Maintenance/ Cleaning Crew had pulled up outside and they all poured in and proceeded to mop and paint and buff and spray, like a little army of Domestic Elves.

It was pushing 4:00 P.M. now. And I knew they'd all be off duty in an hour or so. And I hit the sack and fell asleep to the *whirrrrr* of the floor buffing machine and the reek of Pine-Sol and ammonia.

When I awoke it was dark but I had no idea what time it was. I did not dare turn on the lights in my room. So, taking my now un-frozen pizzas under my arm I headed for the third floor lounge.

Slowly I crept, step by step. And I could not help but notice the whole freaking place was immaculate. I had *never* seen it this clean. The tiled floors just sparkled. The windows were smudge-less. Fresh paint fumes filled the air. Even the bannisters were polished and smooth.

The kitchenette in the third floor lounge had a stove, a sink, and a few cabinets. And for some reason it was all painted orange. I do not remember anyone ever actually *using* this stove. Not once. I pre-heated the oven to 400 degrees and figured while it was warming up I could grab that quick shower.

This I did, and it was magical. I washed away the residue of the Honey Tree—the bacon grease and egg yolk and cigarette ashes and gravy lumps. I washed away my eviction for cause and the cold damp nights on the road or by the river. And for the first time in days I was mildly content.

And then the fire alarm went off.

Actually, the fire *alarms* went off.

I think every fire alarm in the whole damn building went off.

After my mild heart attack I slipped into my 501s and red hooded sweatshirt and raced upstairs to the third floor lounge.

And my god, I have never seen so much smoke in my life! Curling, deep black, acrid smoke hung three feet down from the ceiling! It was a cloud of doom! It churned and rolled like demonic thunderheads!

Nice, I thought, *I am burning down my dormitory. This will make Southwestern College History. I've gone from bending the rules a tad to Felony Arson.*

And *then* I noticed something.

They say where there is smoke there is fire. But *there was no fire.*

And, despite my panic that I had to get the hell out of there, my adrenaline-stoked synapses started firing and I figured it all out pretty damn quick.

Yes—the maintenance crew cleaned the walls and the floors and the windows.

Yes--they polished the doorknobs and scoured the toilets and shower stalls.

Yes—they dusted out the cubby-hole mailboxes and the wiped all the Naugahyde lounge furniture clean as a whistle.

But? *Did they clean the fucking stove?*

Nope.

From the amount of black smoke pouring out of that oven like locomotive breath, I'd bet my almost-cowboy-hat that stove hadn't been cleaned in *years*. And when I fired it up just ten minutes earlier it went off like a hot tar kettle.

Relieved the dorm would live to see another day, I turned off the oven, opened every window I could on that floor and got the hell out of Dodge about a minute before the fire trucks arrived.

Reid Hall was right on the edge of campus so I was walking very nonchalantly down the darkened Winfield Streets in no time at all, with just my wallet and the clothes on my back.

Nonchalantly isn't really the right word. I was pissing my pants. And I wondered if the Winfield City Police could lift fingerprints off of a soggy pizza.

At *least* I was not in jail.

That would come later.

That very night.

And it would have *nothing* to do with dorm-sneakery and a filthy old stove.

CHAPTER 12

HOP, SKIP AND GO DIRECTLY TO JAIL

Did you ever wake up somewhere and *not know* where you were?

I did.

Did you ever wake up somewhere and not only not know where you were *but how you got there?*

I did.

Did you ever wake up somewhere and not know where you were or how you got there but also had a black eye, broken ribs and clothing torn to shreds?

I did.

Did you ever try to put together a 500 piece Jigsaw Puzzle that was *entirely white* and all the edges of the pieces were soft and pliable as cookie dough...*blindfolded*?

I did.

Did you ever learn a life lesson so profound that 44 years later it is still a viable ratchet in your toolbox of life?

I did.

And here is how:

From the minute I woke up the morning after I almost burned down Reid Hall at Southwestern College, I found myself both the sole suspect and the sole detective in a mystery yet to be solved. So, as my Uncle Donald Palmer (New York City Gold Shield Detective) once told me, "Start with the facts and work backwards."

So, walk backwards with me, please.

FACT: Just a few moments after awakening, my eyes still not adjusted to consciousness, I stood up and walked directly into something very, very hard. They were the cold, gray, steel bars of a jail cell.

The sleuth in me naturally ascertained I was in jail. Now, I had never been in jail before, but it didn't take a Gold Shield Detective like Uncle Donald to realize that is *exactly* where I was. It was cold and gray and dark and there were these bars. Ergo...

FACT: The door to my cell, however, was wide open. Therefore, I assumed that whatever I had done to deserve incarceration was a misdemeanor, at best. But, *crap*, I must have done *something*.

I yelled *HELLO* and my words echoed throughout the small cell block. After a few seconds a Winfield City Police officer walked through these two big metal doors and said

"Well, look who's alive."

He then proceeded to fill in some of the gaps in my memory, which were legion. All I knew at the moment is that my ribs hurt so hard that every breath I took was like an ice pick in my side; that I had a shiner the size of a tennis ball and my left eye was completely shut and congealed in dried blood; and that my 501s and my red hooded sweatshirt had been torn up pretty damn bad and were covered in crusted mud and still aromatic vomit.

Good Morning, Douglas Scott Delaney.

The Police Officer led me out of the small cell block and into the office where he poured me a cup of black coffee and had me take a seat. He then placed a form inside his manual typewriter, scrolled it in, looked me dead in the eye and said, "Name?"

And I said, "Doug Delaney."

"*Ahhhh,*" he said, "the hitcher?"

And I said, "Yes."

Apparently, word of myself and my booby-trapped Spring Break adventure had trickled through the Winfield P.D., due to my first two encounters with them earlier in the week. This would be my escort out of town and my warning about vagrancy upon my return to town just one day later.

"You got any I.D.?" The Police Officer said.

I reached for my wallet, which was gone, and said, "Don't you have it?"

And he said, "Nope. When we found you, you had no I.D. on you."

FOUND ME?

You *FOUND ME?*

Did someone leave me on your doorstep in a wicker basket with a note? Did they ring the bell and run away? I'm a fucking *foundling*?!

According to this Police Officer I was *found* face down on the concrete walkway in Memorial Park at about 2:30 A.M. This is a small municipal park dedicated to Veterans of W.W. I. It was right there on 9th street in Winfield, across from Wheeler's I.G.A.

And I was out cold.

According to the Police, I was "already pretty beat the hell up."

But when they nudged me to see if I was indeed somewhat alive, I apparently leaped into that "Fight or Flight Mode."

And I chose *FIGHT*.

It seemed that *whoever I must have had a fight with* some time earlier that evening was still fresh in my memory as I actually started swinging at the police as if they were my combatants.

This is *never* good idea, but in my defense I had neither the intention *nor* the memory of swinging at the police. I was simply out of my mind. And *why was this?* Well, more backward detection is needed to answer that question.

"Am I under arrest?" I asked the Police Officer.

"No," he said. "We brought you in for your own protection."

"Protection from who?" I said.

"We're not sure," he said. "But mostly from YOU."

FACT: At approximately 2:30 A.M. (a few hours earlier) I was discovered by the Winfield City Police Department Graveyard Shift, passed out at the base of the Veterans of W.W. I Monument, after a concerned citizen had called in and said something to the effect that "There's a dead guy in the park." After being resurrected by said W.P.D. Officers, they muscled me into their cruiser and then, obviously, to jail, where apparently I wasn't much of a threat because they didn't even shut the cell door.

After the officer took down some more information, he pulled the form out of the typewriter and said, "Come with me."

He led me to the parking lot behind the station where a police cruiser was parked. He pointed to a huge dent in the rear passenger side door.

"Look familiar?" he said.

"Not really," I said.

"You did that," he said.

It was a really BIG dent.

"Me?" I said. "How?"

"You kicked it," he said.

He then led me back inside, where I assumed some kind of charges would be administered.

"Do I need to call a lawyer?" I said.

"No," he said. "You can go now."

He handed me a yellow manilla envelope and inside was exactly $8.25 in quarters.

"Sign for this," he said. "You had no wallet on you. But these coins were in your pants pocket."

We walked to the front glass doors of the W.P.D. and I turned to the man and said

"Thanks."

And he said, "You won't thank me when you get the bill for that door."

7:00 A.M. I was free. *But free from what?* I was already late for work washing dishes down at the Honey Tree. But I couldn't go in there looking and smelling like I did. There was a laundry-mat on the West side of town just across Main Street, and I figured that was job one.

It was still really early and no one was in there so I stuffed my jeans and my socks and my hooded sweatshirt in the washer and I sat in my underwear on an orange, molded plastic chair with an old newspaper across my lap, hoping to hell *nobody* would come in to do their laundry in the next half-hour or so.

Having escaped any severe charges just minutes earlier I didn't want to be hauled back into jail for Public Lewdness.

And as I watched the spinning, sudsy clothes through the washer porthole window, the water turning a nasty brown, I tried to piece together all I could from the night before. And here is what I can tell you:

FACT: After I left Reid Hall, (that oily black oven smoke billowing out of the third floor windows) I walked the darkened back streets to Ninth and McCabe. There was a supermarket there called Boogarts which I hoped was still open, having left my two unfrozen pizzas in the kitchenette back at the dorm. I was just starving.

They *were* still open and, knowing I'd probably be spending the night back down at Tunnel Mill Dam, I loaded up on cans of sardines and Vienna sausage, a few cans of Coke and some chips.

I was checking out when I heard, "Hey, Delaney! What're you doing in town?"

It was Darrell Drennan. And he was toting several bags of tortilla chips and dips. Darrell and his brother Doug both attended Southwestern College. These were lineman-sized guys. And we all played football together. They lived in town over by Wheat Road, so they just stayed in Winfield on Spring Break. They were good friends, always cheerful and helpful. They had another brother named Dave, who was also playing collegiate football but over in Missouri. Anyway, I was damn glad to see Darrell.

Without mentioning the over-sized smoke bomb I had recently and inadvertently set off back on campus, I explained to him why I was still in town and asked for a ride down to the dam. And Darrell said

"Screw that. You ain't gonna' sleep down at the dam. You're coming with us."

"Us" was Darrell and a couple of his buddies (locals whom I did not know) who were waiting for him outside in the Boogarts parking lot. They were headed to a party. A keg party, and I went right along with them.

At this point I have to tell you something: Before this night I had been to one Keg Party in my life. This was in my Senior Year in high school back in Levittown, N.Y. These were usually held on Saturday nights, the day of a Football Game. We called them Victory Parties whether we won or not.

I went to *one* of these. And I brought a six pack of Coca Cola. I just didn't drink in high school. I may have had a total of three beers my entire senior year.

That being said, when I arrived at Southwestern College, I was still 17 and would be until the end of October. I could not legally go to *Joe's City Cigar Store*. While all the legal kids went to the bars on Wednesday and Saturday nights, I sat in the dorm. Occasionally, a sympathetic gal or pal would come by 206 East, Reid Hall, with a six-pack after the bars closed.

Even after I turned 18, and I *could* get into *Joe's City Cigar Store*, if I had three or four beers the entire night it was a lot. Not because I was a goody-two-shoes, but, frankly, because I was always broke.

The extent of my drinking up until this very night was a few bottles or glasses of 3.2. beer a couple of times a week. I had never tasted wine, whiskey, rum, rye, vodka…none of it. The point is, I was not a big drinker at all.

FACT: We arrived at this keg party, which was at a townie's house. I remember the name of the kid hosting this shindig, but in the interest of civility I will just call him Willie. Willie had a *nice* house, filled with antiques and fine furniture, and this place was packed inside and out.

There must have been 60 or 70 people there, locals who were back in Winfield because they went to school out of town. And Darrell seemed to know all of them. And his brother, Big Dave, who was the size of small truck, was there, too. I probably only knew five or six of these folks. And they were having a great time.

Kegs were tapped and there was a circular horse trough, 6' around and 2' deep, filled with ice and what looked like about 1000 bottles and cans of beer of all kinds. There were several folding tables loaded with snacks and soda and a couple of big orange Gott "Gatorade" coolers with spigots on the bottom, next to which stood stacks of (yes, really) Red Solo Cups.

The stereo was blasting *ZZ Top* and *Fleetwood Mac* and *Marshall Tucker* and *Jethro Tull.*

And Darrell led me over to one of those orange Gott coolers, grabbed a Red Solo Cup, and filled it up with this stuff that looked just like pink lemonade. And Darrell said

"Try this."

And I did.

And not only did it *look* just like pink lemonade, it *tasted* just like pink lemonade. And I downed it in a few gulps and poured me another and that is when Darrell said, "Whoa, you better go easy on that stuff."

And I said, "It's just lemonade."

And he said, "No, it *ain't*. It's *Hop Skip*."

And I said, "It's *lemonade*."

And Darrell laughed a big hearty laugh, his big toothy grin shining. And he said "Some people call it *Hop, Skip and Jump*. Some people call it *Hop, Skip and Go Naked*. It's *loaded* with Everclear."

And I said, "What's Everclear."

And he said, "A kind of liquor."

And I was thinking: if *this* is what liquor tastes like, it really isn't so bad. And I had another, and another…

What Darrell *didn't* expound upon was exactly what kind of liquor this Everclear was. I will leave that up to *Wikipedia,* which states:

FACT: "EVERCLEAR is a brand name of rectified spirit (also known as grain alcohol and neutral spirit). It is made from grain and is bottled at 120, 151, 189, and 190 U.S. proof (60%, 75.5%, 94.5% and 95% alcohol by volume, respectively).

Due to its market prevalence and high alcohol content, the product has become iconic, with a '*notorious reputation*' in popular culture. Sale of the 190-proof variation is prohibited in some states, which led EVERCLEAR to start selling the 189-proof version.

According to the manufacturer, EVERCLEAR 'should be viewed as an unfinished ingredient', not consumed directly in undiluted form."

In short, EVERCLEAR is colorless…odorless…jet fuel.

And *that,* me Buckos, is what I was slamming down, Red Solo Cup after Red Solo Cup, while stuffing my face with BBQ chips and onion rings and chili dogs and…

And *this* is where my facts got off the train.

Because the very last thing I remember before waking up in that jail cell was Big Dave Drennan picking me up like a Rag Doll, throwing me over his shoulder and carrying me across the lawn.

Back at the laundry-mat I slid into my now dry and toasty 501s, my ripped red hooded sweatshirt, my tube socks and my Frye Boots. And I headed to the Honey Tree. I knew they would be pissed that I was almost two hours late but after "losing" my wallet and loading the washer and dryer I now had six dollars in quarters in my pocket and I needed that $1.50 an hour more than ever.

I was hoping that when the folks at the Honey Tree took a peek at my shredded clothes and my bruised and battered body I might get pass due to pure sympathy, and that worked. The girls were all over me.

"Sweet Jesus, what happened to you?"

"Oh, you poor baby!"

"Do you need a doctor?"

"Lord! Child! I'll get an ice bag!"

I reveled in that. But all I could offer up for an explanation was, "I zigged when I should've have zagged."

And then I put on my apron and went to work.

Frank was already half in the bag and was popping a fresh Colt .45 oil can when I walked in and he didn't even seem to notice me. All he said was

"You're fucking late, College Boy."

And for the next three days I worked my shift. I took my cash at the end of the day. I slept atop the picnic table down at Tunnel Mill Dam. And on Sunday, the dorms at Southwestern College re-opened and I let myself into Room 206 East, fell into bed and slept for about 17 hours.

My journey was at an end.

But you don't want to hear that. You can't be left hanging like this. This story can't end like *Duel* or *The Birds* or *Picnic at Hanging Rock*. You want to know…nay, you *need* to know what *exactly happened* between unceremoniously leaving Willie's keg party and when the Winfield City Police scooped me up off the pavement in front of the W.W. I Memorial.

And the truth is this:

Using my Uncle Donald's backwards fact finding method I was able to ascertain (over the course of several months, mind you) *exactly* what happened that night.

CHAPTER 13

MAMA TOLD ME NOT TO COME

Over the next several months I was Sam *damn* Spade, piecing together a tattered quilt of coincidence, thuggery and dysfunction....one tiny patch at a time. I picked up blurry snap shots of fleeting moments about that infamous night from the Drennan boys, from the police, from my combatant Keg Party Willie himself, and from just sitting silently at *The Pub* and *Joe's City Cigar Store,* eavesdropping on the locals.

The puzzle was coming together.

It was not complete, but it was as complete as could ever possibly be.

That rubbery, all-white jigsaw was coming together with just a few blank spots. But it would have to do. I knew *most* of it. But that knowledge was not enough to assuage my shame and confusion and hunger for justice.

I was 18 years old, almost 6' tall, 184 pounds of youthful, solid muscle and I played outside linebacker for Southwestern College with reckless abandon and...

I wanted *revenge.*

I *really* did.

And I would exact that in some small way.

But most of all I wanted to know the truth. Because I did not want to live the rest of my life with this black hole of *dumb* nagging at me every time I stepped outside my dorm room.

And this what I uncovered:

FACT: At some point at that keg party myself and the host, Willie, had come to some sort of disagreement. Even he could not recall why. Most likely it was over my hat or my accent. But, who cares? This led to a bit of a tussle, not so much a fight but more a drunken grappling match, which we somehow carried *inside* his house. There we both teetered and fell, destroying one *really expensive* antique chair.

FACT: This little spat was rekindled back outside in the yard, at which point Big Dave Drennan said, "The hell with this shit," and tossed me over his shoulder and carried me back to Darrell's rig and tossed me inside, saying, "You leave this car and I'll break both your legs."

FACT: At this point I did *not* have a blackened eye. I did *not* have busted-up ribs. I had *not* thrown up all over my clothing and said clothing was not torn and soiled. I *also* had my wallet.

Darrell would later tell me, "We felt really bad about the Hop Skip. We just wanted you to sleep it off and we were gonna take you back to our house. *But when we went to leave you were gone.*"

So where did I go? Who did I fight with? Where was my wallet?

FACT: Me being innately stubborn, I was not going to stay in Darrel's rig after Dave planted me there. But, not wanting to incur the wrath of Big Dave again, I simply left, and headed toward Tunnel Mill Dam to call it a night. I basically was being as responsible as I could considering all the damn Everclear I had consumed without knowing it. But, being saturated with that particular poison I headed in the wrong direction. I went South toward the W.W. I monument instead of North toward Tunnel Mill Dam.

FACT: Along the way, a group of brothers (and I *know* their names, too, but will not share that info) found me wandering along the street down by the park. These brothers (whom I will refer to as *The Three Ronzoni Boys)* were notorious around Winfield for various unacceptable behaviors which seemed to be a family kind of thing. They were always in trouble with the cops and, much like Teresa's brother Snaggy-Do, were *go-to suspects* when petty crime and misdemeanors were committed. And I did not know that or even *them* at the time.

FACT: They pulled up alongside me in a sputtering old El Camino. They wanted money and I wouldn't give it to them. And that is where my ass-kicking commenced. Some have said I started that row, but I *know* I didn't. I *never* started a fight in my life. But it doesn't matter because the end result was the same: I was beaten to a pulp, I was robbed, I stumbled into the park, I threw up and passed out.

And there it was.

So simple in its banality.

I had gotten mugged by the Ronzoni Brothers.

I'd been walking the streets of Brooklyn and New York City by myself since I was eight or nine and never once even came close to being mugged. I had to travel 1500 miles from home to become a victim. And that was an eye-opener.

And that is all I got for you.

I wish I could impart some wisdom unto you regarding my *look for America* excursion, but I really can't. I've been *looking for America* ever since those crazy April days so long ago. I have been in 48 states and countless cities and even more small towns and hamlets and though I have *seen* America I have never *found* it. We seem to pave over ourselves and reinvent ourselves and come together and drift apart so often it'll make your head spin.

And it does mine.

All I know is that when I started this story I promised myself I would just try to do what Hemingway advised and *"tell people what happened and what the weather was like."*

And I hope I have succeeded in that.

If not. Well…crap.

But at least I can leave you with these closing notes:

NANCY MATHEWS (who kick-started the whole disastrous shebang) is alive and well and living somewhere in Oklahoma, damn her pretty little eyes. We are good friends and do keep in touch. A few years back (and about 40 years after the fact) Nancy confided in me why she broke up with a day before Spring Break. She said she thought I was going to propose to her and when I didn't she said, "*To hell with him.*" Such, as I have explained, was my knowledge of women and what they might want back then. And to this very day.

BIG DAVE DRENNAN never intended to break my legs at all. He was trying to protect me from myself. Today he is a really excellent woodsmith who has a page on social media called *Shop Drennan* and you should really check it out. Brothers Doug and Darrell are also alive and well. And I miss them and their toothy smiles.

KICKN' K.C. KLOS spent his life in education in the service of Kansas. He has recently retired and taunts me unmercifully by posting all the wonderful places he and his lovely wife have visited around the world, knowing damn well I'll never see these places in person. And that A+ I promised him on that term paper? He got a D. I owe the poor bastard $50.00 but he'll never see it. And ever now and then I feel really, really shitty about dropping those bitchy little June Bugs down his underwear.

THE WINFIELD CITY POLICE DEPARTMENT never did send me a bill for seriously damaging their cruiser. I figure they thought I had been through enough. Looking back, the way they handled me in all three of our encounters that fateful week was with fairness and even kindness. I wish them well.

TERESA (my long cool Ark City Blonde) and I actually dated for a couple of years and she, too, is a great friend to this day. She became an Arkansas City Police Officer and then went on to private security. I can still see her, arms akimbo, rather impatiently waiting for me to respond to *"Can I take you home?"*

EVERCLEAR Since that night at Willie's keg party, I will not and have not consumed proofed liquor of any kind. That is the ratchet in my toolbox. That is a gift. That shit will ruin your life.

SOUTHWESTERN COLLEGE The statue of limitations on setting off fire alarms on the campus of S.C. and within the city limits of Winfield, KS has long since expired, but I did not escape unscathed for my indiscretion that smoky evening. It did not take a genius of a maintenance man to figure out it was *me* inside the dorm that night, and I was brought up on charges before the Student Judiciary. My defense was as absurd as it was desperate. I was patently guilty, but I argued that *if they had just cleaned the damn oven once in a while* none of this would have happened. Much to my own amazement, I was acquitted.

I hope the rest of the people I have introduced you to have lived long and healthy and prosperous lives, or have died peacefully and without pain or want: Beulah, the girls at the Honey Tree, Joe Steiner, Marlboro Man, The Bubbas, Truman, Henny Krug, Lou Mignone, the Bruner Brothers, Jim Stinson, and even the insufferable Frank.

But I hold *no such magnanimity* for the Ronzoni boys.

I hope all three of those little pricks led miserable and unreclaimable lives. I hope all of them had kids just like them and that their beat up El Camino is still their go-to mode of transportation. Actually, I only hope that for *two of them.*

Because, *one of them* was on receiving end of a revenge served cold.

And it was served by me. And though it definitely was revenge, I would like to delude myself into thinking it was a reasonable form of justice delayed.

October 9ᵗʰ, 1981. The Pub, Winfield, KS

I was at *The Pub*. And the Ronzoni Brothers were there. In fact, they were *always* there and I knew that. This was their joint. They ran it like the Sopranos ran the *Badda-Bing*. And there were sometimes more than just the three of them. On any given night there could be six or seven Ronzonis shooting pool and playing darts and generally getting piss drunk. And though I *knew* who they were, and I had seen them since 1978 several times a week, they never did put it together that *I was the guy they robbed and beat the hell out of that night.* I could sit next to them at the bar or at a table and they *never* knew it was me.

And that indignancy only fueled my rage.

For three and half years I had been plotting some kind of retribution, like an assassin…coldly, efficiently, playing all the angles and considering all the repercussions. I knew I could never take on the whole clan. I had to separate one from the herd. I had to be quick and decisive. And I had to be unseen.

Just *give me one damn Ronzoni*, I had dreamed.

And that night, I got one.

And I chose the drunkest one.

Right around 11:30 that night the Ronzonis, townies and frat kids were having a time. It was pool tournament night and the place was packed. And all were plastered. I sat in a dark corner at the back of the bar, in the shadows, near the men's room, like a brooding hitman. The juke box was blasting *Three Dog Night.*

Mama Told Me Not To Come.

The bathroom was way in the back of the bar, just two steps from the rear door which led to an alley which was always dark. And I sat there and waited for a Ronzoni, *any* Ronzoni, to wobble his drunken ass that way and enter that bathroom alone.

And one did.

And I slid in behind him as he unzipped his pants, sighed and began to pee.

I then grabbed him by the waist and the inner thigh, turned him upside down and shoved his head in the toilet.

He was not amused.

I pulled him up a second later and dropped him on the floor as he gaped like a grounded carp and then I washed my hands. As he spit up toilet water and tried to right himself, I placed my Frye boot on his chest and pushed him back onto the filthy linoleum. And I said

"*Remember me?*"

And he said, "No, *dude*." He said "dude" in a manner that was pathetic, as if I were his *friend,* as if it would ingratiate myself to him.

And I said, "Think about it."

Then I ducked into the alley and around the block and walked into *Joe's City Cigar Store* and ordered a frosty cold fish bowl. *Joe's* was quiet. Just a few snooker players and kids playing the Playboy pinball game. Joe Steiner was already wiping down the bar and stocking the bins for the next day. And I ran my finger through the icy cold frost of that fish bowl and had to smile to myself. I had exorcised at least one demon in my life, and there would be more to come. But at that moment I was on top of the world, grinning like a jaybird and saying nothing.

And now, having cleansed my memory banks of that one horrible night three and a half years earlier, my mind flashed free and expansive.

And I decided right there and then I would embark on *another journey.*

I decided I would forsake any further revenge or retribution stemming from my quest *to look for America.*

I decided I would discover Casey, instead.

I would find my raven-haired, tight-jeaned Highway 160 Cowgirl whenever and wherever I would find her. I would hitch-hike or drive the blue highways and the dusty gravel Kansas back roads for as long as it took until I ended up at the foot of her driveway, and then the gate to her corral, and then the steps to her battered and creaking front porch.

And I would knock on the door and say, "Hey."

And she would open the screen door and say, "Hey."

And I would never be afraid of horses ever again.

ABOUT THE AUTHOR

Shown here wearing the infamous *Hat of Contention,* Douglas Scott Delaney is a published and produced writer of fiction, non-fiction, drama and screenplays. Among his many awards are New York's *Broadway Tomorrow Award* and *Los Angeles Critics Drama-Logue* for his plays *Lafitte!* and *My Last Confession.* His screenplay for the film *All Roads Lead Home* was the recipient of the *Los Angles Family Film Festival's* award for best picture. His non-fiction expose, *Tower Dog: Life Inside the Deadliest Job in America* is required reading at The University of Alabama. For further reading visit his website http://www.delaniac.com (where you can also order either hard copies or e-books of his extensive catalog.)